European Union: Deeper Integration or Wider Membership?
– A Multivariate Statistical Analysis –

EUROPEAN UNION: DEEPER INTEGRATION OR WIDER MEMBERSHIP?
– A MULTIVARIATE STATISTICAL ANALYSIS –

ANCA CARRINGTON

Nova Science Publishers, Inc.
New York

Senior Editors: Susan Boriotti and Donna Dennis
Coordinating Editor: Tatiana Shohov
Office Manager: Annette Hellinger
Graphics: Wanda Serrano
Editorial Production: Vladimir Klestov, Matthew Kozlowski and Maya Columbus
Circulation: Ave Maria Gonzalez, Vera Popovic, Luis Aviles, Raymond Davis, Melissa Diaz and Jeannie Pappas
Communications and Acquisitions: Serge P. Shohov
Marketing: Cathy DeGregory

Library of Congress Cataloging-in-Publication Data
Available Upon Request

ISBN: 1-59033-602-X.

400 Oser Ave, Suite 1600
Hauppauge, New York 11788-3619
Tele. 631-231-7269 Fax 631-231-8175
e-mail: Novascience@earthlink.net
Web Site: http://www.novapublishers.com

Printed in the United States of America

To my husband, Simon.

CONTENTS

List of Tables

LIST OF FIGURES

ABBREVIATIONS

BENELUX	Belgium, Netherlands, Luxembourg
CA	cluster analysis
CAP	Common Agricultural Policy
CCA	canonical correlation analysis
CEE	Central and Eastern Europe
CEECs	Central and Eastern European Countries
DA	discriminant analysis
EC	European Communities
EC6, EC9, EC12	European Community of 6, 9, 12 member states
ECB	European Central Bank
EEC	European Economic Community
EFTA	European Free Trade Area
ERM	exchange rate mechanism
EMS	European Monetary System
EMU	European Monetary Union
EU	European Union
EU15	European Union of 15 member states
FA	factor analysis
KMO	Kaiser-Meyer-Olkin measure
MU	monetary union
n.a.	not available
OCA	optimum currency area
PCA	principal component analysis
SEA	Single European Act

Chapter 1

INTRODUCTION

1.1. MOTIVATION

The complex and dynamic nature of the process of economic and monetary[1] integration in Europe makes it an elusive subject for any analysis which aims to be both comprehensive and systematic.

When confronted with the trade-off between rigour and broadness of scope, a very large proportion of economists researching into this area opt in favour of accurate formal modelling of 'details' and sacrifice thus a glimpse at the panoramic view. Nevertheless, one question remains: how do all these minutely explained aspects interact with each other and with what outcome?

This book is a step towards providing an answer, an attempt to sketch the European picture without sacrificing rigour, while retaining as much of the specific features as possible. Our enterprise is far from perfect, but it offers some valuable insight into the process of regional integration in Europe. Until more comprehensive theoretical (as opposed to empirical) developments will emerge, our work could be described as what Blaug (1992) would call a 'declaration of faith'.

1.2. AIM

For most of the last decade of the 20th century, the attention (and often concern) of both the public and the academic circles focused on two aspects of the European integration project: the introduction of the single currency and the enlargement of the European Union (EU) towards Central and Eastern Europe (CEE).

All the intellectual and political debate was then leading up to the two substantial policy changes. However, since the 1st of January 2002 the Euro became reality in twelve European countries. The deadline for the first round of EU accession by CEE countries (CEECs) is also drawing closer. This change in reality brought along a shift in the focus of published research, away from the theory and empirics of monetary integration towards currency analysis for the new monetary unit[2]. Our centre of attention here is the framework of analysis that prevailed prior to and informed the introduction of the single currency.

From an economic perspective, the basis for the analysis of the single currency is formed by the optimum currency area (OCA) literature, which mainly deals with identifying the country characteristics which either reduce the likelihood of an asymmetric shock or increase the ability to adjust once such a shock has occurred (see Tavlas, 1993 for an overview). Most of the relevant (international macroeconomics, largely) theoretical literature comprises exercises in modelling these characteristics individually. The few attempts of developing a formal OCA model focus on one or two relevant characteristics at a time (e.g., Bayoumi, 1994; Mélitz, 1995a, b; Gerlach, 1995). As far as the empirical studies are concerned, the predominant approach is to address the question of whether the EU is an OCA by comparing the economics of the (12 in most studies) member states to the US and/or Canada, regarded as OCAs simply because they do have a single currency.

The literature on enlargement is less developed. Most studies are empirical, concerned with the European Free Trade Area (EFTA) members joining the European Community, EC (Baldwin, 1992), and are typically country studies (e.g. Brakman and Garrettsen, 1993; Kokko, 1994; Lundberg, 1994; C. Martín, 1995).

On CEE, most of the literature deals with trade models between EFTA and the CEECs (Baldwin, 1993a); between the CEECs and the EU (Buigues and Ilzkovitz, 1992; Hoekman and Djankov, 1996) or remains descriptive, focusing on institutional aspects (Åslund, 1991, Knell, 1995). Attempts to incorporate macroeconomic analysis remain fairly limited in number and scope (Branson and Braga de Macedo, 1995; Baldwin, Francois and Portes, 1996).

To our knowledge, only one pre 2002 paper looks explicitly at the relationship between the single currency and enlargement (Bayoumi and Eichengreen, 1992) and, like the other single currency studies, takes an one-dimensional view, dealing with the incidence of demand and supply shocks across an European Community of twelve member states enlarged to include the EFTA countries.

On this background, our aim is to investigate *empirically* the introduction of a single currency in the EU and the potential enlargement towards CEE, individually and in their interaction. We intend thus to integrate the theoretical developments on regional economic and monetary integration developed before the Euro became reality and use them as the framework for our *exploratory* analysis. More specifically, we search for some preliminary answers to questions such as:

1. Are the objectives of the EU compatible with the policy instruments available (at European and at national level)?
2. Are the European objectives compatible with the national objectives of the EU15 member states?
3. Are the objectives of 'deeper' integration (single currency) and 'wider' integration (enlargement) compatible with each other, given the instruments available?
4. Which are the member states most likely to benefit from the introduction of the single currency and what distinguished between potential losers and potential gainers?
5. Do the existing and the potential EU members belong to different 'natural' groups, determined by their intrinsic characteristics? What distinguishes between such groups?

We remain aware of the difficulties involved in modelling such a comprehensive process and of the limitations our response to them imposes on our findings. The predominant problem faced by anyone attempting a quantitative analysis of the CEECs' economies relates to data (un)availability; this becomes even more severe when trying to include both the EU and the CEECs in the same analysis. Our way of dealing with the frustration brought by incomplete, discontinued, incomparable time series across Western and Eastern Europe consists in applying multivariate statistical analysis to a cross-section for which reliable data could be gathered. This leads to the main limitation of our study: the lack of dynamics. We believe that the time dimension could be easily incorporated once dependable time series would have been built for all countries concerned.

Another limitation is linked to the nature of the statistical techniques employed, which lack in solid significance tests. In the absence of suitable instruments for hypothesis testing, we remain within the bounds of exploratory analysis and simply formulate a number of hypotheses suitable for testing in the more traditional framework of econometric analysis. It is worthwhile stressing that, despite their limited power, multivariate statistical techniques facilitate gaining some insight where traditional econometric is rendered powerless by the lack of suitable data.

Finally, there remains the limitation of working on the thin line between positive and normative economics, inherent to the subject addressed here.

Nevertheless, we do believe that this approach contributes to: first, offering a comprehensive picture of the area of policy choice across Europe; second, formulating specific hypotheses to be further investigated and tested, thus facilitating the consolidation of the theoretical literature on single currency and enlargement and the possible development of a theoretical counterpart to our empirical broad-picture investigation; third, rehabilitating the use of multivariate statistical techniques as a valid instrument of economic analysis.

1.3. Structure

Introduction is followed by Chapter 2, which clarifies the research design, by exposing the methodological aspects involved, justifying the suitability of the statistical techniques applied and presenting the variables and data employed. All the relevant mathematical details are included in a Technical Appendix.

Chapter 3 investigates the compatibility between European and national objectives, and between objectives and instruments at national and at European level, with focus on the relationship between the single currency and enlargement as European objectives.

Chapter 4 looks in detail at the single currency objective, by bringing together the major findings of the OCA literature as a basis for empirically separating the potential losers from the potential gainers at EU level.

Chapter 5 investigates the enlargement objective, looking at the existing and potential EU members in terms of similarity defined by economic, political, social and cultural characteristics.

Chapter 6 presents the policy implications following the findings reported in the previous three chapters, under the scenario of the EU pursuing both objectives in the light of the existing literature.

Finally, Chapter 7 brings together two sets of concluding remarks: on the techniques employed and their suitability for economic analysis, and on our findings related to the single currency and the EU enlargement as EU objectives.

Notes

[1] We use here the terminology already established in the literature, although we regard the 'monetary' dimension as 'economic' as the other aspects of the integration process.

[2] The British Library of Political and Economic science lists in its Bath Information and Data Services (BIDS) over one thousand academic articles on the euro after 1997.

Chapter 2

RESEARCH DESIGN

2.1. ON METHODOLOGY AND METHOD

The decision to be explicit about methodology relates to the need of placing our work in the context of scientific inquiry, given the departure of our analysis from the orthodox line.

The methodological basis of our approach finds its closest reflection in what Machlup (1978) describes as ultra-empiricism[1] - a programme that begins with facts obtained, *inter alia*, by statistical investigation. In a broader sense, our methodological position belongs to the dialectic Hegelian view[2], comprising a mixture of realism and empiricism.

The scientific quality of such a path of inquiry is supported by Nesselroade (1994), who stresses that exploration will remain an integral part of scientific activity '[T]o the extent that building a knowledge base involves both deductive and inductive activities' (p.151).

Moreover, this departure from the mainstream practice is not as severe as it appears. After all, in a phenomenological approach one works 'backwards', starting with the data and ending by constructing a theoretical model that could produce an outcome consistent with the data. While this appears to oppose the typical scientific approach for economics, as Dunn and Maddala (1996) declare, in reality 'many econometric studies are *conducted* in a phenomenological framework, although they are usually *presented* as testing (actually 'verifying') some theoretical model of optimization, since this is the current professional convention' (p.53). Without leading to an immediate fundamental theory, an approach based on exploratory analysis would seem suitable for the practical level at which most of the world operates and could point the direction for what may ultimately be a more basic theory.

The suitability of the exploratory approach pursued rests on its ability to offer a comprehensive and comprehensible picture of the process of economic and monetary integration in Europe, process whose complexity, dynamic and lack of precedent make it an elusive target for formal modelling. We follow here Friedman's view (1994)[3] regarding the vital importance of 'full and comprehensive evidence on the phenomena to be generalised' for constructing hypotheses (p.187).

Furthermore, the formulation of strictly empirical hypotheses on the basis of our empirical analysis may contribute to eliminating the weakness of the empirical foundations of economics Fox (1997) warns against.

We are aware of the observational equivalence pitfall, namely that if one hypothesis is consistent with the available data, then an infinite number of hypotheses are also consistent with it and the final choice among them rests on 'arbitrary criteria of 'simplicity' and 'fruitfulness' (Friedman, 1994).

It is not our intention to undermine the importance of models with *a priori* specified functions in the study of subsets of interactions for which the theoretical background is reasonably developed. We only argue that the proposed empirical procedures may prove more fruitful than hypothesis testing for the initial exploration of the comprehensive interactions involved in European integration which, by crossing disciplinary lines, involve relationships about which very much less is known. Our approach should be regarded as a complement and not as a substitute to the usual structured techniques of economic analysis.

The exploratory analysis of statistical data depicting real phenomena leads to findings that have to be tested and modified whenever new data becomes available. As Machlup (1978) points out, while the selection, collection and organisation of empirical data will be influenced by the constructs and deductions of the theoretical system, the particular relationships between these data by means of correlation analysis and other statistical techniques are not deducible from high-level assumptions and can neither confirm nor disconfirm such assumptions. Nevertheless, these relationships, especially the numerical estimates of parameters, coefficients, or constants, are themselves subject to verification by new observations. Tests on the robustness of such empirical findings can strengthen the confidence with which one formulates hypotheses to be tested and incorporated into formal developments in the literature.

All this being said, we sustain that the results of our analysis can suggest hypotheses designed to abstract essential features of complex reality, and thus consolidate the basis for the further theoretical development as far as regional integration is concerned. This is in line with Kaplan's (1964) argument that '[A]s evidence accumulates in support of a theory, we simultaneously come to a better understanding both of the world and of our own ideas about the world' (p.65)[4].

Now let us have a closer look at the proposed method. The European integration process represents a complex phenomenon that entails transformations at economic, institutional, social, cultural and political level.

However, the mere acknowledgement of the role played by non-economic factors does not help much in shifting the knowledge barriers on the issue.[5]

Attempts to introduce non-economic elements in the study of economic and monetary integration in Europe have been widely directed towards the use of political variables, mainly in the literature on monetary policy (and inflation) in relation to central bank independence (e.g. Cuckierman, Webb and Neyapti, 1992; Alesina and Summers, 1993; Alesina and Roubini, 1994).

There remains a whole range of other variables (social, cultural) whose impact on the course of regional integration in Europe has been acknowledged but not fully investigated. Our aim is to include (as many as possible of) these variables in a quantitative analysis framework designed to explore the structure of the underlying forces at work in shaping the progress of European integration.

As Adelman and Morris (1971a) pointed out, the appropriateness of the statistical methodology used in studying a given set of phenomena should be assessed against the kinds of statistical and computing techniques available, the state of knowledge in the relevant substantive field, and the nature of the available data.

Among all these factors, the constraint imposed by data availability plays a determinant role in our choice of technique. While the economic literature investigating the EU uses widely quantitative analysis (mainly time-series regression analysis), the research on the CEECs is mostly left at a descriptive stage[6]. Two explanations spring to mind when faced with these divergent approaches: first, the reservation upon the relevance of mainstream economics to the analysis of the CEECs' economies; second, the fact that the traditional econometric approach is rendered irrelevant (by notoriously unreliable statistical data prior to the 1989 change in the political regime) if not entirely inaccessible (incomplete or non existent/unreported data)[7] when dealing with the ex-communist countries.

The analysis-of-variance group of techniques that we employ are most suitable in dealing with multidimensional phenomena and have been widely used in medicine, sociology, education, biology, meteorology, environmental studies, geology, psychology and sports and, to a lesser extent, in business and economics (Johnson and Wichern, 1992). Considering their increasing popularity due to their ability in dealing with the greater complexity of contemporary research (Tabachnick and Fidell, 1996), our area of interest here provides a good opportunity of extending the use of such techniques to economics research.

The scope for hypothesis testing within this group of techniques remains seriously limited[8]. However, there is considerable reliability as far as hypothesis-making is concerned (Krzanowski, 1996).

2.2. Statistical Techniques

As far as the statistical techniques[9] employed are concerned, our main interest here is in revealing their intuitive appeal in addressing the questions we are interested in. These are, as presented in Chapter 1, the following:

1. Are the objectives of the EU compatible with the policy instruments available (at European and at national level)?
2. Are the European objectives compatible with the national objectives of the EU15 member states?
3. Are the objectives of 'deeper' integration (single currency) and 'wider' integration (enlargement) compatible with each other, given the instruments available?
4. Which member states are most likely to benefit from the introduction of the single currency and what distinguished between potential losers and potential gainers?
5. Do the existing and the potential EU members belong to different 'natural' groups, determined by their intrinsic characteristics? What distinguishes between such groups?

The first three questions can be addressed by the use of canonical correlation analysis (CCA). Canonical correlation is a tool suited for research situations where each subject (country, in our case) is measured on two sets of variables (instruments - objectives; European objectives - national objectives). The aim is to find out if and how the two sets relate to each other. The technique differs from multiple regression in that it allows for several left-hand side variables[10]. Chapter 3 presents the answers CCA gives to questions 1, 2 and 3.

The fourth question calls for a technique enabling the classification of the EU15 member states into potential losers and potential gainers on the basis of their intrinsic characteristics and the identification of those characteristics that have the largest contribution to separating losers from gainers. A most suited technique for this purpose is discriminant analysis (DA), which uses linear combinations of a collection of variables (country characteristics) to distinguish among mutually exclusive groups (losers – gainers) and to identify the variables that are important for distinguishing among groups (Norušis, 1994). The outcome of the application of the technique to country characteristics identified by the OCA literature are reported in Chapter 4.

Finally, the fifth question can be approached effectively by exploration through a combination of cluster analysis (CA) and DA. The purpose of CA is to identify homogenous groups or clusters of objects (countries) on the basis of sets of characteristics and (dis)similarity measures built upon them. Group membership for individual countries and the number of groups are not known *a priori*. Once the groups are empirically identified, DA can be employed once more in order to distinguish those features that differentiate mostly across groups. Chapter 5 reports the findings of the analysis based on this technique.

In each case one needs to clarify the variables to which the techniques are applied (instruments, objectives, costs and benefits from the single currency etc.). As it will become clear in the following chapters, almost all relevant elements are not directly observed; instead, they are identified through measurement on several of their manifestations. Obtaining one unique measure for each variable is made possible by factor analysis (FA), whose aim is to discover which variables in a set form coherent subsets that are relatively independent of one another. The factors extracted summarise patterns of correlation among observed variables (manifestations, characteristics) and reduce a large number of observed variables to a small number of factors (composite measures). Section 2.3 develops further the idea of composite measures and their use in the context of the present study. The actual constructed variables are presented at various stages in the following chapters, as they become relevant.

All empirical results reported have been obtained in SPSS.

2.3. The Variables and the Data

Besides the objective limitations, such as the restrictions related to data availability already mentioned, the selection of the relevant variables to be included in the analysis entails a high degree of subjectivity which, although it cannot be entirely eliminated, can be reduced, and hopefully minimised. One can deal with this problem by selecting those characteristics for which the current literature (on economics, sociology and political science) together with *a priori* reasoning, as well as descriptive historical studies, establish a presumption regarding their impact on the progress of economic and monetary integration in Europe.

At every stage of the analysis we distinguish between 'variables' and 'factors' or 'constructed variables'. The former correspond to data series, quantitative and qualitative, reported in various statistical sources and traditionally used as regression analysis variables (e.g., population, consumer price index etc.), while the latter are built by us (through FA) as composite measures of various concepts not directly measurable (e.g., European identity, labour mobility etc.). Although the 'constructed variables' become 'variables' in further analyses (CCA, DA, CA), we shall refer to them as factors, so as to maintain consistency and clarity.

The analysis covers 38 countries: the 15 EU member states, 21 CEECs, whether they have or have not yet formally expressed their interest in EU membership, as well as Cyprus and Turkey[11]. Given the large number of variables employed (135), we shall not enter into their detailed description (see the Data Appendix for variable definition and sources). However, we are confident that the account of the factors extracted, at each stage of the analysis, will provide sufficient information to help understanding of the way they were constructed.

The main advantage of our approach is the ability to incorporate non-economic characteristics in an analysis which, by using wide cross-sectional data, can cover not only the EU countries, but CEECs as well. We are inclined to use here the argument put forward by Adelman and Morris (1970a) in defence of their pioneering work, which largely inspired us, by saying that the biases introduced by the omission of the influence of institutional, socio-cultural and political phenomena 'on the assumption that they remain unchanged or vary within a limited range only are considerably graver than any biases produced by the inaccuracies of measurement inherent in exploratory attempts such as ours to treat them systematically' (p.662). This is highly relevant given the importance of such elements for the transformation undergone by the ex-communist countries. The accumulation of data with the passage of time will allow for the introduction of a dynamic element into the analysis, making it easier to reassess the role played by economic as well as non-economic elements.

While the use of cross-sectional data surpasses the problems connected with time series data for the CEECs, it is open to criticism as to the static character of the analysis[12]. One way of attenuating this shortcoming is to use of averages for a number of years rather than annual levels, whenever possible. On occasions, data on certain characteristics is not available for the same year for all the countries. In such situations, data from a year as close as possible is being used[13].

The data we use comes partly from official sources (mainly international statistical yearbooks) and partly from opinion surveys. Where data is not accessible or performing a certain measurement for the countries included in the sample is technically unfeasible, we opt in favour of using results of previous empirical studies reported in the literature.

Prior to the analysis data screening has been performed, with special focus on missing values, outliers and normality[14]. The most prominent remains the problem of missing data on several variables, mainly for the CEECs. One obvious solution in dealing with this problem is to delete those observation and/or variables where data is missing. Considering the fact that when missing values are scattered across variables and observations deletion amounts to a substantial loss in the sample size, we used this alternative when no other solution was available (e.g. for Malta). A compromise solution is to insert a sample mean for the missing value. The price of thus maintaining a large number of observations and variables is a loss in variance (since the mean used as a substitute is probably closer to itself than the missing value it replaces) and therefore in the correlation with other variables (see Tabachnick and Fidell, 1996; Little and Rubin, 1987).

The data is standardised with mean zero and unit standard deviation, as to eliminate any bias from the use of various size and units of measurement.

With all this in mind, we can now turn to the first exploration, that of the relationship between policy objectives and instruments within and across the EU.

NOTES

[1] See Blaug (1992) for a comprehensive exposition.

[2] See Reuten (1998) for further references.

[3] The quote comes from the reprint of Friedman's 1953 essay.

[4] To quote Tukey (1980), '[N]either exploratory nor confirmatory is sufficient alone. To try to replace either by the other is madness. We need them both' (p.23). See also Nesselroade (1994) on the interplay between exploratory and confirmatory approaches.

[5] See Eichengreen and Frieden (1993) for a proposal to integrate economic and political elements at theoretical level.

[6] Trade models (e.g. Baldwin, 1993a) and, more recently, macroeconomic simulations (Baldwin, Francois and Portes, 1997) are the exception.

[7] See, e.g., C. Martín (1995) and Lavigne (1995) on the issue of data availability.

[8] Preliminary work on inference procedures in multivariate statistical analysis opens the area to future hypothesis testing; see Gouriéroux, Monfort and Renault (1995) on asymptotic inference and Rubin and Stern (1994) on 'Bayesianly approach' on dynamic factor analysis; less optimistic prospects for cluster analysis in Jolliffe, Jones and Morgan (1995).

[9] A brief introduction to the mathematical treatment of each technique is contained in the Technical Appendix.

[10] Multiple regression is actually a special case of CCA, which is one of the most general of multivariate techniques (Tabachnick and Fidell, 1996).

[11] Lack of data on most variables for Malta prevented us from including it in the analysis.

[12] Papagni (1992) avoids this problem by using three-mode principal component analysis, which takes into account the time dimension. Lack of sufficient/suitable data prevented us from adopting this solution.

[13] As Stone (1951) pointed out, '[I]n practice one does not as a rule have the information one wants but something rather different, with the consequence that tedious and uncertain adjustments, if not wholesale guesswork, must be made in order to estimate what is required. This state of affairs is such a commonplace that it comes in for far less criticism than it deserves' (p.10).

[14] For an overview of the possible ways of dealing with the initial examination of data see Chatfield (1985). See also Krzanowski (1996).

Chapter 3

EU: OBJECTIVES AND INSTRUMENTS

3.1. OBJECTIVES, OLD AND NEW

Regarded at the outset as a stage on the way to political union[1], the creation, nearly fifty years ago, of Euratom and the European Economic Community (EEC) marked in fact the beginning of a period of progressive economic integration. The maintained focus on the political relevance of various economic transformations led, however, to a less than smooth progress. The evolution of the integration process in Europe has been marked constantly by the need to choose between *deeper* integration (further transfer of authority at European level) and *wider* integration (enlarging the 'club', accepting new members)[2].

The acuteness of this problem of choice has been increased by the collapse of the communist bloc in 1989. According to Urwin (1991) this 'had sharpened all the old debates that have plagued the EC over decades: integration or enlargement, intergovernmental cooperation or supranationalism, national sovereignty or federalism' (p.244).

We start the empirical investigation of this deeper vs. wider trade-off by seeking answers to a few related questions: Can the EU achieve its objectives, given the instruments it can use? Are these European objectives in contradiction with the national ones? Can the EU successfully pursue both the introduction of a single currency and enlargement towards CEE?

The Treaty of Rome[3], art. 2, states that the task of the European Community shall be achieved by establishing a common market and an economic and monetary union and by implementing a set of common policies and activities. The task itself is defined, in the same article, thus:

> '...to promote throughout the Community a harmonious and balanced development of economic activities, sustainable and non-inflationary growth respecting the environment, a high degree of convergence of

economic performance, a high level of employment and of social protection, the raising of the standard of living and quality of life, and economic and social cohesion and solidarity among Member States'.

More than a customs union and a common agricultural policy, membership of the EEC also implies commitment to the free movement of both capital and labour, a common investment policy, and the coordination and rationalisation of social welfare goals. Art. 3 lists the activities referred to in art. 2, namely:

(a) the elimination as between Member States of custom duties and quantitative restrictions on the import and export of goods, and of all other measures having equivalent effect;
(b) a common commercial policy;
(c) an internal market characterised by the abolition, as between Member States, of obstacles to the free movement of goods, persons, services and capital;
(d) measures concerning the entry and movement of persons in the internal market [...];
(e) a common policy in the sphere of agriculture and fisheries;
(f) a common policy in the sphere of transport;
(g) a system ensuring that competition in the common market is not distorted;
(h) the approximation of the laws of the Member States to the extent required for the functioning of the common market;
(i) policy in the social sphere comprising a European Social Fund;
(j) the strengthening of economic and social cohesion;
(k) a policy in the sphere of environment;
(l) the strengthening of the competitiveness of Community industry;
(m) the promotion of research and technological development;
(n) encouragement for the establishment and development of trans-European networks;
(o) a contribution to the attainment of a high level of health protection;
(p) a contribution to education and training of quality and to the flowering of the cultures of the Member States;
(q) a policy in the sphere of development cooperation;
(r) the association of the overseas countries and territories in order to increase trade and promote jointly economic and social development;
(s) a contribution to the strengthening of consumer protection;
(t) measures in the spheres of energy, civil protection and tourism' (Rudden and Wyatt, 1994).

Art. 3a.1 specifies that these activities shall include 'the adoption of an economic policy which is based on the close coordination of Member States' economic policies, on the internal market and on the definition of common objectives, and conducted in accordance with the principle of an open market economy with free competition' (Rudden and Wyatt, 1994, p28).

The concept of political union that prevailed in the early days, although permanent in the European debate, remains vaguely defined and reflects a less successful development. The slow progress on the political integration front was, according to Vanthoor (1996), induced from the start by the fundamental difference of opinion between the UK and the Scandinavian member states on the one hand and the rest of the EU on the other regarding the extent to which the transfer of national competences to a supranational authority had to be accepted.

The advance of political integration aside, the process of economic integration among the member states allowed the EC to present a united front in its external relations. As far as the rest of the Europe was concerned, the EC managed to strengthen its connections to EFTA, while failing, for decades prior to the collapse of the Communist regime, to reach any effective agreement with Eastern Europe.

The focus of the late 1980s and early 1990s was on deeper integration, concentrating on the original goal of a common market set out in the Treaty of Rome and on a shift in the existing balance of power away from the member states towards the Community institutions[4], within the framework of the 1986 Single European Act.

The commitment to the completion of the common market objective by 1992 resuscitated the interest of the EFTA countries in EC membership. For them, the relevant problem was the one of the trade-off between political commitment and economic development. As for the EC, the choice was to be made between further integration and enlargement, the pressure increasing with the collapse of the communist bloc and the re-emerging prospects of a genuine pan-European union.

The outcome was, under Delors' active leadership, a strengthened commitment to integration, the objective of European Monetary Union (EMU) becoming again the main topic of debate.

The close coordination of monetary policies has a long tradition among the member states, although the provisions included in the Treaty of Rome on this matter were rather brief[5]. During the first 15 years of the EC the early steps in this direction were taken while the Bretton Woods system was providing exchange-rate stability and a basic framework for policy coordination. The turmoil in foreign exchange markets in the late 1960s enhanced the desirability of stable exchange rates among the EC members, as a requirement to preserve the successful achievement of establishing a customs union and Common Agricultural Policy (CAP). As a reaction to the intensified political pressure on the Community generated by the collapse of the old monetary order, the need for monetary union (MU) was increasingly recognised and regarded as a way to enhance the process of economic and political integration in Europe. This materialised in the Werner Plan adopted in 1970, in which the irrevocable fixing of parities and the total liberalisation of capital movement by 1980s were envisaged as a way to create the EMU.

However, the international and financial disorder of the early and mid 1970s[6] proved that the first European exchange rate arrangement (the "Snake") set up in 1972 was unable to provide a proper framework for the coordination of monetary policies in Europe. This brought the process of monetary unification to a halt, the stagnation lasting until the European Monetary System (EMS) came into being in March 1979.

The Community efforts to complete the "Europe 1992" programme gave a new momentum to the process of monetary integration, the objective of MU becoming the driving political force to obtain economic integration. Thus, the adoption of the Delors Report in 1989 as the official blueprint for monetary unification was followed in 1991 by the decision on the timetable and convergence criteria to be met prior to the establishment of the European currency union, taken by the European Council at its Maastricht meeting in December 1991.

Art. 3a.2 of the Treaty includes on the list of the 'activities' required for the fulfilment of the common objectives 'the irrevocable fixing of exchange rates leading to the introduction of a single currency, the ecu[7], and the definition and conduct of a single monetary policy and exchange rate policy the primary objective of both of which shall be to maintain price stability [...]' (Rudden and Wyatt, 1994, p28).

The economic preconditions for EMU membership are detailed further in the protocols attached to the Treaty (known as the Maastricht criteria): for one year prior to membership the inflation rate should be less than 1.5% higher than that of the three best performing member states; for one year prior to membership, long term interest rates should be less than 2% higher than those of the three best performing member states; for two years prior to membership there should be no devaluation within the narrow band (±2.25%) of the exchange rate mechanism of the EMS; a national budget deficit of less than 3% of GDP; a public debt of less than 60% of GDP (Rudden and Wyatt, 1994). The Stability and Growth Pact that ensued from the European Council meeting held in Dublin in December 1996 sets the ground for ensuring continuing budgetary discipline in the final stage of EMU.

From 1st of January 1999 the Community moved to a single monetary policy and a single currency, under the monitoring of the European Central Bank (ECB). Following a more or less strict compliance with these carefully set and much debated rules, the new currency began its circulation on the 1st of January 2002 in twelve EU member states. As The Economist (2001) points out, its arrival marked an important new phase of Europe's long term integration that started with the 1986 Single European Act and the 1992 single market project.

The accession of new members represented a feature of the EC from its inception: the legal framework set in art O. of the Maastricht treaty (replacing the original art. 237), provides that every European country may apply for EU membership.

The rules of accession relate primarily to the obligation of the new comers to accept fully the *acquis communautaire* (the EC legislation, institutional structure and modes of behaviour) as well as the *finalité politique*, the ultimate objective of political union (Winters, 1993).

From the incumbents' perspective there is no unique reason behind the decision to accept new members. Successive waves of enlargement rested on a mixture of reasons: economic mainly[8] in the case of the addition of the UK, Ireland and Denmark in 1973; predominantly political[9] for the second wave, bringing in Greece in 1981, Portugal and Spain in 1986, as well as for the 'back door' enlargement brought by the 1990 German unification; mixed, with the inclusion of the ex-EFTA members, Austria, Finland and Sweden in 1995[10].

As far as the CEECs are concerned, the growing interest of the EU to support their efforts towards integration has been reflected in a series of recommendations and decisions adopted by several European Councils during the last decade.

While expressing the intention to accept the objective of the Visegrad group (Czech Republic, Hungary, Poland, Slovakia, Slovenia) regarding membership, at Edinburgh in 1992, at its 1993 meeting in Copenhagen the European Council declared its intention to eventually enlarge the EU eastward, making 'for the first time, eastern enlargement no longer a question of "if" but only a question of "how" and "when"' (Hopkinson, 1994, p.4). The promise was extended to any CEEC with a "Europe Agreement", conceived as a framework within which they can prepare for accession (Baldwin, 1995). At the same meeting, a set of economic and political conditions[11] for membership have been agreed upon for the CEECs. The economic elements of the so-called Copenhagen criteria relate to: i) the existence of a functioning market economy; ii) the capacity to cope with competitive pressure and market forces within the Union; iii) the ability to take on the obligations of membership, including adherence to the aims of economic and monetary union (Daviddi and Ilzkovitz, 1997).

Four years after Copenhagen, Agenda 2000 assessed the readiness for membership of ten CEECs and declared five of them in compliance with the criteria (Czech Republic, Estonia, Hungary, Poland and Slovenia), while calling for the Community institutions to help the remaining five (Bulgaria, Latvia, Lithuania, Romania and Slovakia) meet the conditions required for starting the accession negotiation early in the next century.

The 1999 Helsinki summit recognised thirteen candidates for membership: six proceeding with full accession negotiations started in 1998 (Cyprus, Czech Republic, Estonia, Hungary, Poland and Slovenia); six expecting full negotiations to start early 2000 (Bulgaria, Latvia, Lithuania, Malta, Romania and Slovakia) and one with candidate status but no envisaged negotiations (Turkey).

All these discussions prompted more changes to the institutional setting of the EU. The Treaty of Amsterdam, in force since May 1999, gives the legal foundations for the reforms anticipated by the Agenda 2000 and lists among its objectives making the Union's institutional structure more efficient with a view to enlarging the Union (Sverdrup, 2002).

The most recent changes and additions to the EU legal framework were brought by the Nice Treaty, which followed the 2000 inter-governmental conference, aimed at reviewing the functioning of EU's main institutions in view of expansion. It is not surprising that, given the scale of change associated with enlargement, this last Treaty triggered a wave of reflection on the wider issues related to the organisation of the EU.

3.2. Compatibility Issues

Let us turn now to the exploration of the relationship between and among objectives and instruments. As Robson (1998) points out, in the case of regional integration blocs, such as the EU, trade-offs are to be expected as far as the attainment of different objectives by member states and the bloc is concerned. Policy optimisation takes place in a broad sense, within the integrated area.

The traditional approach to the relationship between policy instruments and objectives is the one initiated by Tinbergen (1952). It mainly consists in finding the numerical values of the instrument variables as functions of the targets and certain structural data and indicating the relationship between these functions and the structure of the economy. This is usually done while assuming as given the structure of the economy, the target variables and their numerical values, as well as the nature of the instrument variables.

Broader and therefore more constructive for our purpose is the approach developed by Adelman, Geier and Morris (1969) who attempt definitions of the two categories of variables, using their characteristics. Thus, specific to target variables or goals is that 'they reflect fundamental positive changes which increase the effective range of choice of the individual members of the population with respect to their economic, social and political actions and they can only be measured and implemented indirectly' (p.411). On the other hand, instruments 'are more or less directly manipulable by national governments and are generally regarded as desirable primarily because of the ends they serve' (p.411).

In the analysis that follows, we are departing from Tinbergen's line, since we are not concerned with building a macroeconomic model designed to analyse the relationship between the goals and instruments of economic policy by formulating a preference function for the decision-maker together with a structural model of the economy. Instead, we follow an exploratory approach, along the lines of the work of Adelman and Morris (1965, 1970a, 1970b, 1971a, 1971b, 1973), Adelman, Geier and Morris (1969) and investigate the degree of compatibility between the European objectives and the instruments available through CCA applied to variables obtained through FA. The relevant details of the quantitative analysis are given in Chapter 2 and the Technical Appendix.

Using art. 2 of the Treaty of Rome as the starting point, we identified the following set of European objectives and instruments, along with their national counterparts:

Table 3.1: Objectives and Instruments

	Objectives	Instruments
European	• European integration and identity • standard of living • single currency • price stability • enlargement to CEE	• single market • political power centralisation • media support (expectations) • fiscal policy
National	• standard of living • employment • national integration and identity • democracy • growth • welfare • political stability	• education and literacy • factor endowment • government intervention • media (expectations) • investment • foreign trade

There are two main problems one encounters when attempting such identification and quantification of objectives and instruments: first, the subjectivity involved in measurement (mainly in relation to the selection of variables to be included in FA); second, the static set-up of the analysis. The latter limitation is of particular importance in the case of the EU, for which the frontier between instruments and objectives is not an immutable one. For instance, two decades ago, the single market was an objective; since 1992 it became an instrument in the pursuit of growth and development objectives. The single currency had the status of objective over the last decade, while the EMU is, from the perspective of Agenda 2000, an instrument to be used towards enlargement[12].

The former limitation is addressed here by using the prevailing view in the literature devoted to the EU as guide in the choice of variables. Given that our primary aim here is to explore the relationship between the single currency and enlargement as objectives of the EU, we deal with the latter problem by consistently working with the grouping defined in Table 3.1.

Before we can proceed with the analysis of any such relationship, we need to obtain some measurement of these objectives and instruments. For each of them we can find a number of quantitative manifestations. Each group of such variables can be compacted in one single measure, by an application of FA.

The information contained in 105 variables (comprising economic, social and political characteristics, as detailed in the Factors Appendix) has been extracted in 33 factors reported in Table 3.2, which summarises their statistical properties. The factors have been obtained in 21 separate rounds of FA. The reported values for the Bartlett test are used in relation to the null hypothesis of identity correlation matrix. The test evaluates all factors together and each factor separately against the hypothesis that there are no factors. This is rejected (at the 5% level of significance, for most factors), indicating that there are common factors in the variables included in each extraction. This finding is supported by the high KMO parameters and the large percentage of the total variance explained by the factors extracted (both mostly over 0.5 and, for some factors, over 0.75).

Specific to this type of analysis is the sensitivity of the results to the variables included. Our main concern here is to reflect as much as possible the meaning and importance attributed *a priori* to each variable, rather than purely optimise the statistical properties of the results. For this reason we maintain the reported specification[13].

Let us take a closer look at two factors: F15 (national identity) and F16 (national integration). For the first one there are four variables with estimated coefficients above the 0.5 cut-off limit. (The values of the estimated parameters are reported in the Factors Appendix). Among these, three are positively related to F15, namely: the percentage of population feeling attached to one's country (V60), the percentage of population belonging to the predominant religion (V14) and the percentage of population speaking the national language (V13). Meanwhile, the factor is negatively related to the percentage of population in favour of a federal EU (V61).

Table 3.2: Composite Measures - Tests of Significance

Factor		Bartlett test[a]	KMO[b]	% of total variance explained
F1;	-investment in human capital (education expenditure);	42.77140	.51932	**68.5**
F2	-human capital potential (enrolment ratio);	(.00336)		
F3;	-government intervention (European dimension);	21.65669	.54203	**75.9**
F4	-government intervention (domestic dimension);	(.01695)		
F5;	-media penetration (national);	34.35718	.62213	**85.3**
F6	-media use (national);	(.00016)		
F7;	-media penetration (European);	20.72265	.75384	**75.8**
F8	- media support (European);	(.02311)		
F9;	-actual investment;	14.09358	.41439	**81.5**
F10	-investment potential;	(.02861)		
F11	-EU trade;	46.60981 (.00000)	.66647	**68.5**
F12;	-standard of living (urban life);	45.41560	.38604	**63.6**
F13	-standard of living (health);	(.45463)		
F14	-(un)employment;	13.96931 (.02998)	.69063	**58.2**
F15;	-national identity;	19.03621	.49700	**67.6**
F16	-national integration;	(.21210)		
F17	-democracy (national and European level);	10.34154 (.11099)	.42815	**47.3**
F18;	-sustainable growth (from technological change);	31.91763	.61817	**73.2**
F19	- sustainable growth (from income);	(.27788)		
F20	-military expenditure (trade-off to welfare);	15.43752 (.01711)	.67888	**70.3**
F21;	-government stability;	72.93590	.45794	**58.1**
F22	-ideology;	(.64090)		
F23;	-European identity;	25.00405	.38527	**60.4**
F24	-European integration;	(.24699)		
F25;	-Eastern enlargement (expectations);	6.38866	.48190	**56.0**
F26	-Eastern enlargement (attitude);	(.97245)		
F27;	-single market (cultural integration);	22.57668	.31846	**61.1**
F28	-single market (freedom of movement);	(.75392)		
F29	-political power centralisation (European institutions);	127.00440 (.00000)	.78001	**81.3**
F30	-fiscal policy;	6.29778 (.09799)	.51989	**58.2**
F31	-price stability;	10.93260 (.09048)	.73298	**62.9**
F32	-single currency;	12.80993 (.04616)	.51916	**53.9**
F33	-factor endowment	193.21765 (.00000)	.71007	**76.4**

a - significance levels in parentheses; b - Kaiser-Meyer-Olkin (KMO) measure.

The variables with estimated coefficients above 0.5 and positively related to F16 (national integration) are: transfers from the central government to other levels of national government as percentage of central government expenditure (V33), the percentage of people regarding themselves as 'nationals', as opposed to 'Europeans' (V59), and the percentage of population speaking the national language (V19). The factor is negatively related to the percentage of population belonging to the predominant religion (V14).

This example is somehow peculiar, given the correlation of two of the variables (V13 and V14) to both factors. It is therefore illustrative of the frequently encountered situation of difficulty in interpreting the outcome (in F16, as opposed to F15). We have to note, in this particular case that we have retained as input for further analysis, F15 only.

A more straightforward case is F11, EU trade, which is positively related, with coefficients of over 0.5, to imports from EC12 (V93), exports to EC12 (V94) and the percentage of intra-industry trade with the EC (V89).

We could very well have called this factor EC trade, but we opted for 'EU trade', so as to maintain coherence in referring to the European regional trading bloc. Since FA is not an aim *per se*, the names given to the factors relate very closely to the ultimate purpose of our analysis. We opted for names that fulfil a heuristic function, are mnemonic and suitable for future use in the further analysis, while helping us in maintaining the consistency of result reporting and interpretation[14].

The next step is to use these measures for objectives and instruments and study the way in which they interact, by an application of CCA. We take pairs of objectives and instruments, as outlined in the first column of Table 3.3, which also reports the statistical properties of the estimated canonical correlation functions. Pillai's criterion is a multivariate test available in SPSS and suitable for testing (in small samples) the null hypothesis of zero interaction between the two sets of variables. Note that in four of the five cases the pairs of canonical variates (sets of factors) are significant at the 10% (part A). The finding is reinforced by the high (>0.8) squared canonical correlation coefficients. Note that all the functions explain over 75% of the total variance.

Table 3.3: Canonical Correlation: Tests of Significance

Function	Pillai's criterion[a]	squared canonical correlation coefficient	% of variance explained
part A			
Instruments vs. objectives (national)	1.14813 (.328)	.987	88.666
Instruments vs. objectives (Europe)	1.56055 (.120)	.836	75.168
National vs. European objectives	1.48149 (.122)	.984	92.156
Political vs. economic factors (Europe)	1.66623 (.068)	.991	83.339
Political vs. economic factors (national)	2.03387 (.030)	.999	97.194
part B			
Instruments vs. objectives (national)	1.17830 (.295)	.987	91.934
Instruments vs. objectives (Europe)	1.85750 (.120)	.836	75.168
National vs. European objectives	2.50624 (.041)	.984	93.021

[a] -significance levels in parentheses

We investigate the robustness of our findings by altering slightly the set of variables (factors) employed. The starting subset included for the estimation of the canonical functions comprised the first (largest eigenvalue) factors extracted. Augmenting these subsets in a stepwise procedure, by introducing the 'second' factors (where two factors have been extracted, as reported in Table 3.2) did not increase the significance of the canonical correlation and thus only the results based on the first factors have been retained. Also, part B in Table 3.3 reports the statistics corresponding to the canonical correlation estimated excluding the political factors (F21, F29). The marginal differences between the parameters indicate robustness of the results reported in part A.

We can now proceed to the interpretation of the estimated correlation parameters. In analysing the outcome of CCA we concentrate on the relationship among variables with estimated parameters of at least 0.5 and/or statistically significant at the 10% level. The parameters reported in Table 3.4 measure the correlation of each variable to the canonical variate other than the one it belongs to (e.g., between each instrument and all the objectives).

The first column lists the couples of variates analysed. Their ingredients, the variables, are listed by their factor codes in the next column.

Instruments *vs.* objectives at national level: The first function indicates a high compatibility between (in decreasing order of size of the structure coefficients): media penetration/expectations (F5), EU trade (F11), investment in human capital (F1) and factor endowment (F33), on the one hand, and sustainable growth (F18) and standard of living (F12), on the other hand.

Moreover, as far as the objectives are concerned, a trade-off[15] can be identified between growth (F18) and standard of living (F12), as opposed to national identity (F15) and military expenditure (F20).

Instruments *vs.* objectives at European level: The achievement of the European objectives depends mainly on the success of the single market programme (F27) and, again, the shaping of expectations through media (F7). The use of fiscal policy (F30) appears to be negatively related to the objective of Eastern enlargement (F25), along with the maintenance of the standard of living (F12), while supporting the single currency (F32) and price stability (F31) objectives.

Therefore, it appears that the achievement of national objectives is not intrinsically related (or dependent upon) the main attributes of national sovereignty. Note also that the coefficient on government intervention (F3) is very small.

Table 3.4: Canonical Variates: Structure

Function	canonical variate 1			canonical variate 2		
	variable	correlation	significance	variable	correlation	significance
instruments	F1	.699	.036	F20	-.430	.505
vs.	F33	.438	.684	F15	-.572	.114
objectives	F3	.064	.674	F12	.713	.104
(national)	F5	.895	.001	F14	-.854	.034
	F9	-.223	.323	F17	-.407	.242
	F11	.740	.099	F18	.889	.004
				F21	.302	.719
instruments	F31	-0.53	.247	F27	.546	.200
vs.	F23	-.323	.657	F29	-.116	.269
objectives	F25	.768	.024	F7	.939	.008
(Europe)	F12	.601	.074	F30	-.435	.290
	F32	-.686	.066			
national *vs.*	F20	.743	.003	F31	0.94	.001
European	F16	.342	.249	F23	-.053	.789
objectives	F14	.983	.000	F25	-.261	.602
	F17	-.015	.847	F12	-.442	.031
	F18	-.687	.049	F32	.982	.000
	F21	-.303	.787			
political *vs.*	F15	.217	.207	F11	.495	.004
economic	F3	-.897	.003	F1	-.337	.007
factors	F5	.215	.013	F9	.506	.291
(national)	F17	.136	.401	F12	.009	.024
	F21	.171	.624	F14	.273	.081
				F18	-.366	.002
				F20	.320	.666
				F30	.695	.021
				F33	.595	.008
political *vs.*	F23	.189	.862	F11	-.906	.005
economic	F25	-.102	.007	F12	-.648	.121
factors	F27	.027	.094	F14	.824	.000
(Europe)	F7	.545	.014	F30	-.023	.101
	F17	-.194	.285	F31	.790	.004
	F29	.546	.006			
	F32	-.825	.000			

These findings are in line with the prevailing views in the literature. On the one hand, the original EU fiscal transfers system could not cope with an enlarged group of countries, where all new members would be net beneficiaries. On the other hand, as the OCA arguments show, fiscal transfers are essential to the smooth functioning of a monetary union.

As far as the objectives are concerned, there appears to be a trade-off between single currency (F32) and Eastern enlargement (F25), as well as between Eastern enlargement (F25) and the maintaining of a European identity (F23).

It should also be noted that the centralisation of the political power at the European level (F29) appears to play no major role in the achievement of the common objectives. This is consistent with the view that the European institutions in their actual setting are inappropriate for the tasks set (rather than being of no use whatsoever), a problem addressed by the 2000 inter-governmental conference.

National *vs.* European objectives: As for the compatibility between national and European objectives, the single currency (F32) and price stability (F31), at European level, depend mostly on employment (F14) at national level. In turn, employment (F14) has a positive relationship to military expenditure (F20) which is, however, negatively related to growth (F18). On the other hand, the trade-off between single currency (F32) and enlargement (F23) is again present. This time, however, enlargement (F25) has a very small coefficient and so does European identity (F23).

This could be regarded as an indication of the need to address (un)employment problems at national level prior to the move to the single currency. Interestingly enough, unemployment did not appear among the Maastricht criteria, nor is it part of the Stability and Growth Pact.

Democracy (F17) and government stability (F21) seem to play a marginal role when the connection between the national and European objectives is considered.

Political *vs. e*conomic factors: At national level, there is indication of a negative relationship between the degree of government intervention (F3), on the one hand, and European trade (F11), investment (F9), resource utilisation (F33) and fiscal policy (F30), on the other hand.

Note that media (F7), national identity (F15), democracy (F17) and government stability (F21) have small coefficients. The same is true for the standard of living (F12) and employment (F14), while investment in human capital (F1), growth (F18) and military expenditure (F20) are only marginally relevant.

Thus, the use of government authority at national level undermines, among other things, the success of the fiscal policy which, in turn, is compatible to the single currency (see above).

At European level, the centralisation of political power (F29) combined with a favourable shaping of expectations (F7) appear to be conducive to price stability (F31) and employment (F14).

High levels of trade (F11) and improved standards of living (F12) are positively related to the single currency (F32), regarded as a political rather than economic objective, in this context. As such, and considering the expectations (F7), they are, as anticipated, negatively related to inflation and unemployment.

3.3. SINGLE CURRENCY VS. ENLARGEMENT

Through the application of exploratory multivariate statistical techniques, we found, overall, a significant correlation between objectives and instruments of the EU. We also found a similar overall relation between national and European objectives.

However, some indication of trade-off is present across such objectives and instruments. Most notably, the results suggest a possible trade-off between what we called the 'new' objectives of the EU: introduction of a single currency and enlargement towards the CEECs. One should regard such an outcome with due caution, given the strong element of uncertainty implied by the *ex-ante* measurement of the two objectives. Moreover, part of the information on which the factor extraction for these two objectives has been based reflects expectations and attitudes with respect to the introduction of the single currency and the enlargement towards the CEECs. To the extent that these attitudes and expectations can be regarded as anticipating consistent forthcoming policy changes, one could regard the identified trade-off as circumstantial evidence of a trade-off between the two objectives.

This would imply that, if they were to pursue both objectives at the same time, the EU member states would have been likely to accrue larger costs than if they were to focus on one objective at a time. As the experience of the last decade shows, the choice was made in favour of the single currency, which was keenly pursued while the issue of enlargement remained largely one for negotiation.

It is beyond the scope of this book to measure the extent of such negative externalities across objectives. Instead, we turn to a detailed discussion of each of these objectives, before moving on to an exploration of the emerging policy implications.

NOTES

[1] See Urwin (1991) and Vanthoor (1996) for historical accounts of the process of regional integration in Europe.

[2] Some authors use 'widening' when referring to the scope of the common institutions' powers and 'enlargement' in relationship to membership (see, e.g., Pelkmans, 1998).

[3] The articles we refer to are included in the Treaty establishing the European Community as amended by subsequent treaties.

[4] As well as dealing with measures required by the completion of the common market, the Single European Act also referred to new policy objectives, forms of decision-making and legislative processes within the EC, in the spirit of deeper integration.

[5] Actually, post World War II monetary cooperation in Europe was present prior to the formation of the European Communities: the Multilateral Monetary Compensations Agreement, including France, Italy and the BENELUX countries was in existence in 1947.

[6] This was linked to the collapse of the system of fixed exchange rates in 1971 and the first oil price shock in 1973-74.

[7] The name was subsequently changed to 'euro' by the decision of the European Council at Madrid, in December 1995 (European Commission, 1995).

[8] The first enlargement related relating in principal to the 'concern of lost markets' (Winters, 1993).

[9] The second wave was, according to Winters (1993), meant to secure the newly established democracies.

[10] See, e.g., Baldwin (1992).

[11] These relate to democracy and the rule of law, human rights and respect for minorities (European Commission, 1997).

[12] See Pelkmans (1998) for a detailed account.

[13] We examined the robustness of our findings by reapplying FA to slightly altered sets of variables. On occasions the exclusion of one variable or another marginally improved the statistical results.

[14] See Rummel (1970) for 'hints' on factor interpretation.

[15] Adelman, Geier and Morris (1969) describe the relationship between objectives/ instruments with coefficients of opposite signs as a 'pattern of substitution'.

Chapter 4

SINGLE CURRENCY

4.1. OPTIMUM CURRENCY AREA ARGUMENTS: THE COSTS

The main approach[1] used in identifying and, where possible, quantifying the costs and the benefits of introducing a single currency is the one developed in the optimum currency area (OCA)[2] literature, which deals with the fundamental tradeoff between microeconomic efficiency and macroeconomic stability and identifies the conditions which make a currency area attractive both to the union as a whole and to each of the participating countries[3].

The OCA literature concentrates mainly on the costs of a single currency, on the presumption that the benefits are small and, most important, given the impossibility of comparing the benefits representing a permanent flow to the costs that only follow a specific shock (Mélitz, 1995a). This situation is reflected also in the empirical literature[4]. Neither the costs nor the benefits on their own are sufficient for an evaluation of any policy change. What we attempt here is to bring together sets of measurements on both and to explore the net result, using multivariate statistical analysis, mainly FA and DA.

In assessing the costs (and benefits) associated to the introduction of the single currency we have in view the reciprocal relationship that cost involves. As Samuels and Schmid (1997) put it, '[I]t is often said in an argument that such and such policy will incur a cost, as if the incurring of a cost is dispositive of the issue at hand. Contrary to that happening is the reciprocal nature of cost: if the adoption of policy 1 implies cost, so too does the adoption or continuation of policy 2. The difference has to do with whose interests are to become a cost to whom else' (p.213).

With this in mind, we use as the standard of reference the alternative regime of commodity and factor markets integration (common market) but where the individual countries retain their monetary autonomy, which allows them to adjust their exchange-rates (since the 15% fluctuation band as of August 1993 makes the reference to the ERM practically irrelevant). Our focus is thus on the net outcome from the introduction of a single currency, and not an evaluation/valorization of the costs/benefits involved in absolute terms[5].

Most of the literature devoted to the study of the costs of a single currency is based on the assumption that monetary policy *is* an instrument capable of improving the automatic adjustment mechanism and that, therefore, the absence of an independent monetary policy is costly.

Following Mudell (1961), the basic argument in the literature on OCAs as far as the costs of monetary unification are concerned relates to the inability to pursue independent monetary policies and to use the exchange-rate as an instrument of adjustment when confronted with **asymmetric disturbances**. However, the presence of divergent national interests are not only due to asymmetric shock, as they can also be triggered by common shocks that lead to asymmetric effects because of differing national economic structures (Arestis et. al., 2002).

The magnitude of the losses involved depends on both the incidence of disturbances and the speed of adjustment of the economies involved. However, there are several factors that may moderate the loss of autonomy in monetary policy, making the market forces a substitute for exchange-rate variability.

While symmetrical policy responses are the solution for similar disturbances across regions/countries (eliminating the need for policy autonomy), distinctive national policies are necessary when disturbances are asymmetrically distributed or speeds of adjustment are markedly different across countries. It follows that the more asymmetric are the shocks undergone or the more different are the speeds of adjustment at regional/national level, the higher are the costs involved by the introduction of a single currency.

The nature of disturbances and the ease of response are, certainly, only two of the various factors affecting the outcome of the decision to abandon policy autonomy for a MU. According to Bayoumi and Eichengreen (1994a), if domestic policy itself is a source of the disturbances - due to systematically misuse of the policy by policy-makers - 'monetary unification among countries less susceptible to such pressures may imply a welfare improvement' (p.7).

It follows that the stronger coordination of economic policy among the member states can lead to a reduction in the shocks due to unexpected changes in the national economic policies (i.e. internal shocks)[6]. A similar effect can be expected from behavioral changes (e.g. changes in the investment demand, because of a more integrated goods and factor market) and from changes in the industrial structure (e.g. expansion of intra-industry specialisation). Meanwhile, the increase in the external strength of EU15 can stimulate international coordination and thus cause fewer external shocks (see Hansen, Heinrich and Nielsen, 1992). Frankel and Rose (1998) add to this the support of strong empirical evidence that countries with close trade links tend to have more tightly correlated business cycles.

By closely inspecting aggregate supply and demand disturbances, Bayoumi and Eichengreen (1994a) investigate the suitability of different groups of European nations for monetary unification, identifying countries that experience similar economic disturbances. They start from the idea that monetary policy can increase the speed of adjustment, whether the disturbance represents a supply shock that permanently shifts the long-run equilibrium or a demand shock that temporarily displaces output and prices from invariant steady-state levels. Considering that the larger the disturbances, the more disruptive will be their effects and the bigger the importance placed on instruments (such as monetary policy) that might be used to offset them, countries experiencing large asymmetric disturbances are regarded as unsuitable candidates for forming a MU.

They find that in the EU, where adjustment tends to be sluggish (implying higher costs of monetary unification), Germany and its Northern neighbours (Austria, Belgium, Denmark, Finland, Ireland) display the speediest responses. Interestingly, the region centered on Germany excludes over half of the EC12 members, while including two old EFTA countries, now members of EU15 (Austria and Finland). In other words, the results ignore membership of EC12 (EU15) as formal trading block in Europe (see also Bayoumi and Eichengreen, 1992).

These results support the position of the proponents of two-speed MU in Europe, with France, Germany and the smaller Northern member states (Belgium, Denmark, the Netherlands) proceeding in the fast lane. As Bayoumi and Eichengreen (1994a) conclude, 'a European monetary union might run more smoothly if limited to a subset of EU members' (p.36). Similar findings are also reported in Bayoumi and Eichengreen (1997). Viñals (1996), on the other hand, argues against this finding, by stressing that country-specific shocks are relatively less important than generally believed in driving unemployment and concludes that there is no clear-cut distinction between core and periphery countries.

The view that seems to have been favoured with the introduction of the euro is that of Frankel and Rose (1998) who show that, paradoxically, a country becomes a suitable candidate for monetary integration *ex post*, i.e. once it already is a member of a MU.

Since Mundell published his seminal paper on OCAs in 1961, it became widely accepted that countries between which there is a high degree of **factor mobility** are regarded as suitable candidates for monetary integration, due to the appropriateness of factor mobility as a substitute for exchange rate flexibility in promoting external adjustment[7].

While in the short run the primary component of well-functioning inter-regional payments mechanisms is represented by financial capital flows, labour mobility plays a major role in the longer run, in facilitating adjustment to payments difficulties which are temporary in nature (Tower and Willett, 1976).

As pointed out by McKinnon (1973), this approach is concerned almost exclusively with the geographic factor mobility among regions/countries, ignoring factor mobility among (or within) industries. However, in the case of EU15 the later should also be considered, given the relatively high volume of intra-industry trade for all the member states. Since in the presence of intra-industry trade the adjustment costs in face of asymmetric shocks are lower[8], both regional and intra-sectoral factor mobility could work as a substitute for exchange rate variability.

When, in the presence of an asymmetric shock, labour can move from the depressed to the booming region/country, the need for different policy responses (i.e. the pursuit of independent policies) to prevent the emergence of regional problems is eliminated.

The OCA literature includes a number of studies that aim at measuring labour mobility among and within the EC12 member states (e.g. Eichengreen, 1990a; 1990b; 1993) and comparing it to the US performance, the traditional OCA benchmark. The general conclusion is that under this criterion the EC is less of an OCA than the US, for which there is evidence supporting the role of inter-regional labour migration as a channel of adjustment to shocks (Blanchard and Katz, 1992).

However, these results should be regarded with caution, since due to the differences in the geographic units of analysis, the migration rates might not be comparable. Besides, as Eichengreen (1993) points out, '[L]abour may move less within European countries not because it is less mobile intrinsically but because it has less incentive to move' (p.131).

As far as the labour mobility *among* the European countries is concerned, Gros (1996) reports that international migration amounts to more than two thirds of inter-regional migration and is expected to increase among those member states which have similar diversified industrial structures, once remaining statutory barriers to migration are eliminated[9]. However, this might not be exactly the case if one considers the importance of cultural and linguistic differences among the member states, which could lead to differences in labour mobility among certain groups of countries with relatively lower/higher cultural barriers[10] and the likely social tensions in the recipient countries in the presence of large migration (Goodhart, 1991).

Moreover, one of the arguments of the so-called "new theory of OCAs", derived from the theory of microeconomic decision-making under uncertainty, brings a change in the traditional approach concerning labour mobility: since, under uncertainty, the higher is income variability, the lower is labour mobility, asymmetric terms-of-trade disturbances will lead, through the higher income variability they generate, to lower factor mobility (Tavlas, 1993).

Some would argue that the introduction of the single currency itself will affect labour mobility (based on McKinnon, 1963). It will be interesting to what extent that is the case, once data becomes available.

Besides labour mobility, the response of capital flows to disequilibria is crucially important, since capital is needed to finance investment which, in turn, determines employment through the multiplier process.

Defining a high mobility of capital as 'a high elasticity of substitution, for holders, between assets in one country and assets in another, and, for debtors, between liabilities in one country and liabilities in another', Fleming (1971) argues that its effects in the event of payments disequilibria between the members of the group is 'much more doubtful than in the case of labour mobility' (p.472).

Under the assumption that within the currency area there are no official measures tending to restrict or distort capital flows, capital mobility among member states is likely to mitigate or accentuate the hardship resulting from losing the exchange rate as an adjustment instrument. In the presence of disequilibria related to the current account balance, if the incentive to invest declines less than savings in the high-cost countries and rises less than savings in the low-cost countries, the capital movement in the presence of interest rate differentials will allow the high-cost countries to maintain a higher level of employment and the low-cost country a lower degree of inflationary pressure. However, if the changes in the incentive to invest are larger than the changes in the level of savings, the capital flows will shift in favour of the latter, the attainment of the payments equilibrium being possible with more unemployment in the high-cost countries and more inflation in the low-cost countries. The final outcome depends, according to Fleming (1971), on the nature of the disequilibria, the sensitivity of investment to the level of economic activity and the time period considered. The conditions change once a single monetary policy (and interest rate) replaces the national ones, making relevant the distinction between financial capital (prompted to move by interest rate differentials) and FDI, with the latter expected to continue having an impact on the economy.

As Tower and Willet (1976) argue, although high capital mobility does not represent a perfect substitute for 'efficient adjustment mechanisms', it may 'be of some limited use even in the long-run and it reduces the cost of adjustment both by making it unnecessary to adjust to temporary reversible disturbances and by allowing needed longer-run adjustment to spread out over a longer period of time' (p.29). According to McKinnon (1963), the role of capital movements in promoting efficient economic specialisation and growth is more important among small areas than among large, economically developed areas.

As far as the barriers to capital movements within EU are concerned, the Maastricht Treaty on European Union replaced, as from 1 January 1994, the original EC Treaty provisions, the fundamental rules set out in art. 73b stating that all restrictions on the movement of capital (par. 1) and payments (par. 2) between member states and between member states and third countries shall be prohibited (Usher, 1994).

The limit of the capital mobility argument relates, according to Corden (1994), to the fact that the elimination of a current account deficit through borrowing is financing and not adjustment, and thus it only shifts the costs of forgoing the exchange rate instrument to the future. Therefore, while capital mobility is helpful in the presence of asymmetric shocks, it does not have the same effect in response to an adverse shock that is expected to be permanent or long lasting.

Factor mobility alone does not provide the solution for both internal and external balance in a currency area and, therefore, the assessment of the costs involved by the introduction of a single currency should consider it in conjunction with a variety of other characteristics of the countries engaged in a monetary integration process.

Another element relevant to the costs of introducing a single currency is, as Fleming (1971) puts it, 'the extent to which costs in the various parts of the fixed exchange rate area tend to rise at similar or at different speeds when employment is at nationally acceptable levels' (p.476). From this point of view, **similarity in inflation rates** can be regarded as an indicator of similarity in national employment goals, in rates of productivity growth and in the degree of trade union aggressiveness.

Bayoumi and Eichengreen (1994a) find a high number of significant correlations of inflation across Western Europe. However, when eliminating the part accounted for by the international business cycle, the correlations of inflation across Western Europe show no significant pattern. The profile of inflation across the EU is fairly persistent, with high inflation traditionally associated with the so-called Southern members (Greece, Italy, Spain and Portugal). Despite the warnings from economic theory and the requirements of the Maastricht criteria, all these countries did adopt the euro.

Reassurance comes, however, from some relatively recent contributions to the literature. The time inconsistency issue (Tavlas, 1993) reverses the ordering between similarity of inflation rates and currency area participation. The former is thus regarded as a desirable outcome derived from such participation (since a country's monetary policy credibility can be enhanced when attached to that of a country with a low inflation anchor currency), and not as a precondition, as in the classical approach. Nevertheless, this argument holds true in the long run, while in the short run transition costs will be imposed (in terms of unemployment for the high inflation countries, in terms of difficulties in controlling the money supply in the presence of increased capital inflows, for the low inflation countries).

It is difficult to define *a priori* the duration of the transition period and one can only expect that the progress of the integration process in Europe should bring some light on the issue. However, it can be argued that a long transition period can lead to high costs which can shadow the expected long-run benefits.

The costs (and benefits) of introducing a single currency depend also on the **openness and size** of the participating states economies, as first pointed out by McKinnon (1963). The argument is that for small[11] countries which have a high ratio of tradable to non-tradable goods, frequent changes of exchange rate would lead to price instability (since the imported goods, whose prices change directly with the exchange rate, represent a large part of the overall price index); therefore external balance could be more suitably achieved through other adjustment mechanisms. In economies which are highly integrated in commodity trade, fluctuations in their private sectors are highly correlated and thus 'there is less need for independent monetary policies within the bloc and a strong case to be made for imposing the uniform discipline that a common currency would provide' (p.85).

Openness can also be regarded as a partial substitute for high elasticities of excess demand and supply in reducing monopoly power and promptly transmitting disturbances, and thereby preventing wage and price divergence tendencies, capable to forestall some potential political conflict and enhance the credibility of the currency area arrangement (Tower and Willett, 1976).

Although criticised for allowing only for domestic disturbances (see Ishiyama, 1975), the trade interdependence argument remains widely accepted, along with the idea that the costs of MU decrease and the benefits increase with the intensity of trade within a given geographic area (e.g. Dyson, 1994; Krugman, 1990; De Grauwe, 1997).

The degree of openness varies across the EU15 member states: some member states are characterised by a relatively high exposure to the outside world (Benelux and Ireland), while others are relatively less open (Greece, Italy and Spain). However, for all member states over half of the total volume of trade takes place with other EU member states (Eurostat, 1995; De Grauwe, 1997). A substantial part of this trade is of an intra-industry nature (Baldwin, 1992).

The link between the degree of **industrial diversification** and MU has also been explored. According to Kenen (1969), the likelihood that an adverse shock would have a major impact on an economy will depend to some extent on how diversified is the economy's production structure. Under the assumption that the principal cause of the payments imbalance is represented by microeconomic demand disturbances, substantial exchange-rate variations become less frequently necessary in a diversified economy, because of the averaging of the external shocks.

Insofar as economy-wide disturbances are the aggregates of industry-specific shocks, countries with similar industrial structure are likely to face similar aggregate disturbances. Moreover, when industry-specific shocks are imperfectly correlated, countries characterised by a diversified structure of the economy are likely to experience smaller aggregate disturbances as opposed to countries with highly specialised economies (Bayoumi and Eichengreen, 1994a, 1994b).

This argument has also been criticised, mainly for relying on restrictive assumptions and for failing to identify the critical value above which there is "enough" diversity (Masson and Taylor, 1993). As in the case of the openness criterion, the relative advantages of exchange-rate flexibility depend on both the nature of shocks and on the precise policy objectives.

A general indication on the diversification of domestic production for the EU member states can be obtained from the contribution of the main sectors in total GDP. For all the member states the manufacturing sector represents between 1/7 and 1/3 of production, while the share of primary commodities is relatively small, except for Greece and to a lesser extent for the Netherlands and Portugal (Euromonitor, 1995).

As far as the industrial structure is concerned, De Nardis, Goglio and Malgarini (1996) find that specialisation in Europe is stronger at the regional than at the national level and that, to the extent that asymmetric shocks are mainly regional, the loss of exchange rate as a policy instrument is limited.

When **price and wage flexibility** are present, the adjustment costs in terms of unemployment and/or inflation are eliminated and the need for exchange-rate adjustment diminished. Although the changes in domestic prices and wages are slower than for nominal exchange rates, a strategy of relying on wage and price adjustment avoids the inflationary implications of devaluation, while removing rather than alleviating the relative prices distortion that actually imposes the problem of adjustment.

As argued by Dyson (1994), 'labour mobility or large fiscal transfer mechanisms are less important in so far as wage and price flexibility at the regional level acts as a means of responding to a problem of adjustment' (p.245). Moreover, according to Tower and Willett (1976), wage and price flexibility have the additional benefit of reducing the political friction that arises from the need to settle on an appropriate rate of wage and price inflation for the community as a whole.

However, as Fleming (1971) points out, wage and price flexibility has progressively been reduced in almost all economies by both the growing importance of collective bargaining in the labour market and the natural or state-induced monopoly in product markets.

No hasty conclusion should be drawn, Goodhart (1991) warns, as the loss of independent monetary policy may change the attitude of both parties to the wage bargain who, by realising that the ability to affect national employment is slipping out of the hands of the national authority, might be encouraged to respond more flexibly to local demand and supply conditions, thus improving the working of the labour market.

In the case of the EU, it is relevant to identify the degree of institutional convergence across the member states, given that divergent structures of the labour market can lead to asymmetric responses even in the presence of symmetric shocks and thus increase the centrifugal tendencies and the pressure on the ECB. Some evidence of structural change in (some of) the EU member states over the 1980s is reported in Anderton, Barrell and McHigh (1992).

Analysing the impact of EMU on wage flexibility, the Commission of the EC (1990) concludes that it is largely dependent on both the governments reactions to temporary shocks and the impact of EMU on the expectations of the participants in the wage bargaining process and its effects on real exchange rates, and alleges that 'conditional on such considerations, wage flexibility may be able to substitute for the cushioning effect of the nominal exchange rate instrument' (p. 151).

It seems that the held belief in the EU remains that allowing the participating countries to share a similar experience of price and wage change will lead to similar attitudes toward the optimal inflation-unemployment tradeoff and facilitate agreement about optimal macroeconomic policy, easing the task of the ECB.

The willingness and ability of the members of the currency area to adopt common policies meant to facilitate or reduce the need for adjustment can play a crucial role when the factors affecting the ease of adjustment to asymmetric shocks are not strong enough.

At national level, when labour mobility, industrial diversification and wage and price flexibility are not present to a sufficient extent, the fiscal instrument can be an important substitute for the exchange rate in cushioning individual countries or regions from shocks. In a currency union, however, the suitability of **fiscal policy** in replacing the abandoned monetary instrument is hindered by the free-riding problem. The possibility of member states issuing debt in excess of their ability to service it, forcing other members to bail them out is exactly what the Stability and Growth Pact is trying to prevent. Unsustainable fiscal deficits in one country impose pressures on other countries to subsidise the errant government, either through money expansion, explicit fiscal transfers from other members, implicit interest subsidies, or loan guarantees (Masson and Taylor, 1993). To this should be added the reduced ability to adapt fiscal policy to changing economic conditions, due to political reasons (Bayoumi and Eichengreen, 1994a; Corden, 1994).

Therefore, a form of fiscal federalism, i.e. a system of fiscal taxes and transfers between the members of a currency union, could represent an alternative or complement to larger national or regional deficits and surpluses for shock-absorbing purposes[12]. While most authors agree that a fiscal transfer mechanism implies the existence of some form of political union, there is no agreement on whether such a political union is necessary for the successful operation of currency unions. According to Goodhart (1996), the very existence of a single currency in the EU could help 'to erode national selfishness in a manner that would facilitate the subsequent transfer of suitable fiscal competences to the federal centre' (p.1089) which, he argues, could further serve to support the single currency.

Although the nature of the spillover effects changes in a currency union, the need to internalise the externalities remains an argument in favour of policy coordination. While both a mechanism for fiscal transfer and enhanced policy coordination are helpful in ensuring the fiscal discipline and reducing unfavourable regional effects, the decision to create the institutions of fiscal federalism remains a political choice that sets the loss of sovereignty against shared goals among members.

The cost of losing the ability to pursue an independent monetary policy is expected to be higher if the instrument enables governments to pursue their specific preferences about inflation and unemployment. Following the criticism of Friedman (1968), it became increasingly accepted that the **long-run Phillips curve** is vertical i.e. that money is neutral.

However, the monetary neutrality proposition is weakened by several caveats, including 'the political tensions that emerge in cooperative monetary unions under conditions of asymmetric shocks, the tendency of such shocks to exacerbate the business cycle in the peripheral country in hegemonic unions, and the importance of accounting for such factors as initial positions, endogenous growth effects, the costs involved with imposing legal restrictions and the loss of seigniorage at the national level for countries with an underdeveloped tax system' (Tavlas, 1993, p.681). In other words, there are circumstances when monetary changes would not feed through directly into price changes.

If these arguments are correct, the likely costs involved by the introduction of a single currency are considerably increased, since it involves giving up an instrument which, at least in the short run, proves valuable.

In a currency union the member states' governments will also lose the gains related to the right to issue the national currency. However, due to the international dimension of **seigniorage**, this loss might be compensated by the revenue derived from the use of the single currency as an international currency, which represents a common gain to the union as a whole. With the single European currency becoming a major international currency, there would be possibilities of raising seigniorage from the rest of the world (Alogoskoufis and Portes, 1992). Moreover, there were even expectations that the rest of the world may hold a larger stock of the union currency compared to the combined stock of the national currencies of the union members in the absence of the MU (Hansen, Heinrich and Nielsen, 1992). The loss would be reduced by a transfer of the seigniorage revenue from the union level to the national level[13]. So far the performance of the euro has been contrary to the predictions of its proponents (Arestis et al., 2002).

In practical terms, the introduction of a single currency represented an unprecedented challenge for the European banks, requiring of them a logistical exercise of extraordinary dimensions. Although the **technical costs** involved are related to the transition process and not to the adjustment problems imposed by the replacement of the national currencies of the member states by the single currency, they are extremely relevant, since they are actually the first costs to be incurred by the member states (if one does not regard the pressure put by the Maastricht criteria as costs for the member states in their attempt to qualify for the single currency).

A first attempt of estimating the likely time and cost for banks to introduce a single currency was made by the Banking Federation of the European Union (1995) in a survey launched in July 1994 on over 100 banks around the EU. The minimum cost to the EU banking industry of the implementation of the single currency is estimated to be in the range of ECU 8-10 billion or 5-6% of operating costs spread over 3-4 years (ca. 2% of operating costs each year). Over 80% of these costs are represented, in terms of major functions, by changes to the information technology systems and equipment (over 50%); marketing, public relations and stationery (around 20%) and staff training (around 10%). In terms of major product areas the costs relate to money transmission activities, including international services (around 60%); loans and deposits (around 20%); foreign exchange dealing, treasury management and capital markets (around 20%).

The introduction of the single currency in Europe does also impose costs on the corporate and retail customers of the European banking industry, affects customers' needs after the transition, the market structures and the volume of bank business in the future.

In addition, issues such as opportunity costs, risks or benefits resulting directly from the impact of the change on economy and business environment are to also be considered in assessing the overall costs of the introduction of a single currency.

One should not neglect the **psychological costs** involved by giving up the national currency as a symbol of national identity. The attitude across member states as far as further integration is concerned varies widely, whether it has to do with being in favour of the introduction of the single currency (29% in Denmark to 74% in Italy) or feeling attached to the idea of EU (23% in Finland to 64% in Luxembourg)[14].

Finally, to these one should add the costs implied by the insufficient guarantees for the **irreversibility** of the process, given the present structure of the EU and the fact that 'the sovereign state has ultimately turned out to be a more obstinate phenomenon than it was generally considered to be in the 1950s' (Vanthoor, 1996, p.114).

4.2. Benefits from Monetary Unification

Besides its political significance, the single European currency is an attractive achievement due to the economic benefits it involves.

The expectation of substantial microeconomic gains from the **reduction (or elimination) of exchange-rate variability** is built on the idea that there is a direct relationship between exchange-rate variability and risk in trade and investment. It follows that, by increasing the volume of trade, the stabilisation of the exchange-rate will enhance the standard gains form trade.

At least in theory, the negative impact of exchange-rate variability on trade is stronger when there are no efficient financial markets to allow hedging the risk generated by unstable exchange-rates. However, the hedging operation on the (forward or futures) financial market itself involves both direct costs and opportunity costs in terms of resources immobilised, while the forward and options markets are incomplete in terms of maturity and currencies.

In general, the results of various empirical studies on the effect of exchange-rate variability on trade are not conclusive, most of them failing to find any robust relationship between the two. The situation is similar for the effects of exchange-rate variability on international capital movements[15]. The costs and the availability of hedging instruments appear to be inversely related to the degree of sophistication of financial markets and the size of the firms (Commission of the EC, 1990). On the other hand, according to Eichengreen and Frieden (1993), exchange rate variability may actually promote foreign investment insofar as it does encourage investors to hold diversified portfolios of assets with income streams denominated in different currencies.

For the case of Europe, the expected increase in the volume of trade induced by the elimination of the remaining intra-EMS exchange-rate variability was estimated as less than 1% (Gros and Thygesen, 1992), while the gain of eliminating the residual differences in interest rates as about 0.05% of Community GDP (Commission of the EC, 1990). According to Gros and

Thygesen (1992), the full realization of the benefits of irrevocably fixed exchange-rates remained dependent upon 'the additional step of introducing a common currency to underline the definitive nature of EMU and eliminate the inconveniences that would remain in managing an economically and financially integrated area with separate currencies' (p.249). In their opinion this will more than offset the costs involved by the introduction of a single currency.

However, it should not be ignored that the move to the single currency can only be expected to eliminate the exchange-rate variability *within* the monetary union[16]. Exchange-rate uncertainty will remain in the relationship between the single currency and third currencies and, if the common currency becomes a reserve currency in the world economy (due to the vulnerability to speculative capital movements), it might even increase for the individual member states compared to the situation before the creation of the currency union (Hansen, Heinrich and Nielsen, 1992). Moreover, Goodhart (1991) points out the distinction between the reduction of nominal uncertainty and the comparative movement in relative real (labour) costs and its impact on competitiveness.

The existing estimates of the **gains from risk elimination**, however accurate, are global and do not provide an insight concerning the distribution of such benefits across the EU15 member states. Some insight into country profiles can be based on Hofstede (1990) and his measured uncertainty avoidance index. On this basis, the countries with the highest aversion to risk (such as Greece, Portugal, Belgium, France and Spain) can expect the highest gains, while countries less averse to risk (e.g. Denmark, Sweden, Ireland, UK) would anticipate lower gains from the elimination of intra-EU exchange-rate risk. Note that of this latter group only two countries adopted the euro.

The introduction of a single currency involves significant additional benefits as compared to irrevocably fixed exchange-rates, in terms of **transaction costs** and credibility of the irrevocable commitment to fixed-exchange rates.

The elimination of exchange-rates related transaction costs is actually regarded as the main economic gain from the introduction of a common currency in Europe. These include both direct transaction costs (paid by households and firms to the financial sector as foreign exchange commission and differences between buying and selling rates) [17] and in-house costs (incurred by companies, due to the need to allocate personnel and equipment to foreign exchange management). The estimated transaction costs differ widely across the EC12 member states, being lower for the large member countries whose currency is extensively used as a means of international payments (between 0.1-0.2% of national GDP) and larger for the small open and less developed economies (around 1% of their national GDP) (Commission of the EC, 1990).

According to Gros and Thygesen (1992), the elimination of transaction costs can represent a net gain to society only when the resources - especially personnel - previously engaged in executing foreign exchange transactions will be efficiently employed somewhere else.

It has been suggested by the same authors that, since the direct savings from the introduction of a single currency are of about the same size as the direct savings from the abolition of frontier controls as estimated when evaluating the benefits of the internal market programme, the indirect effects of a common currency could be of similar magnitude as the indirect gains expected from the accomplishment of the internal market programme.

The **elimination of information costs** allows consumers across EU15 to evaluate and compare prices and prevent firms from preserving their local monopoly power and from charging higher prices in the markets where demand is inelastic. As a consequence, the benefits of introducing a single currency go beyond the direct savings in transaction costs.

The welfare effects associated with the introduction of the single currency should include also the increase in transactions to follow. However, within each member state, the increase in efficiency is likely to be accompanied by distributional effects which will not necessarily benefit all economic sectors or groups.

When the time dimension and capital accumulation are taken into account, the **increase in the (marginal) productivity of capital** as an expression of the increase in overall efficiency derived from the introduction of a single currency can be highlighted. As firms respond to more promising and safer investment opportunities within the single currency framework, and due to the more efficient allocation of investment through financial markets free from any residual exchange rate uncertainty, a larger capital stock can be expected to be generated (Gros and Thygesen, 1990).

Since an increase in the (marginal) productivity of capital leads to an increase in investment and, thus, in the capital stock, and since a higher capital stock makes possible more output with the same labour force, the single currency induces a multiplier effect on the initial increase in efficiency. Of course, this gain is to be set against the reduction in consumption associated with the increase in the capital stock.

Another dynamic effect arising from the introduction of a single currency relates to the **reduction in the risk premium** which is expected to stimulate investment and increase output over time, due to the increase in the capital stock. The reduction in the overall uncertainty affecting investment can be achieved through both the elimination of exchange-rate movements and the reduction in the uncertainty about monetary policy when there are no longer distinct national monetary authorities - and, eventually, through a more stable fiscal policy. The estimates of the EC Commission lead to the conclusion that EMU could bring important gains in output if it reduces the overall uncertainty affecting investment in the EU member states. It is also argued that EMU will strengthen the expectations of business leaders that future investments will become more profitable, the move to the single currency could initiate a cycle of increasing investment and lower unemployment (Commission of the EC, 1990).

Although most of the growth models used for the evaluation of the benefits of EMU explain continuing growth as a result of exogenous technological progress, a number of more recent models focus on the importance of the economies of scale and spillovers that arise in the accumulation of knowledge. According to Gros and Thygesen (1992), this approach implies that in the long run, the integration in the knowledge market and not the transaction costs savings (which affect primarily trade in goods) will be the most important source of gains.

The introduction of the single currency also eliminates the need for the national monetary authorities to maintain **foreign exchange reserves** to defend intra-EU exchange rates. It remains the obligation of the ECB to keep reserves for the management of the European single currency against other currencies, mainly the US dollar and the Japanese yen. Moreover, in a currency area with a common pool of external reserves, the disturbances affecting each country's payment balance will, according to the law of large numbers, partially cancel out, making the need for external reserves of the whole area lower than the sum of reserves held previously by the member countries (Tower and Willett, 1976).

In the case of the EU these implicit gains are rather small, since foreign exchange reserves were previously invested in interest-bearing assets, and thus, involved relatively small costs to be eliminated.

One benefit of the introduction of a single currency in Europe that was envisaged from the outset relates to the creation of an European competitor for the US dollar (and the Japanese yen) in the international financial system and eventually partial substitute for the US dollar in global financial investments.

The size of the potential benefits of portfolio substitution depend largely on the elasticity of substitution between assets denominated in the EU15 currency and the US dollar (or other currencies). This follows from the fact that global financial markets will be willing to hold a given supply of assets denominated in the EU15 currency if its interest rate will be high enough. A substantial change is thus anticipated for the international role of the single European currency in its three functions: means of payment, unit of account and store of value (Alogoskoufis and Portes, 1992). As we have already seen, the performance to date of the euro does not match this anticipation.

Although the overall analytical basis developed in the literature does not allow for a proper measuring of the economic benefits from **stable prices** (or, in other words, of the economic costs of inflation)[18], it remains widely accepted that inflation causes considerable costs.

At microeconomic level, the effects of anticipated inflation relate to sub-optimal money holdings, inflation tax and menu costs. While inflation tax and the costs of changing price lists or income-tax schedules are regarded as negligible, the welfare losses from a rate of inflation which is different from the optimal rate appear to be substantial. According to estimates by the Commission of the EC (1990), it is of the same order of magnitude as the transaction costs savings induced by the introduction of a single currency.

The macroeconomic effects of anticipated inflation depend to a large extent on whether the argument of the short-run tradeoff between inflation and unemployment is regarded as valid and the long-run Phillips curve is considered vertical. While it became widely accepted that, in the long run, there is no stable relationship between inflation and unemployment, there is no strong evidence in favour of the vertical long-run Phillips curve either.

Surprise inflation has a stronger economic effect, mainly on government revenues and at the macroeconomic level. The larger potential revenue of surprise inflation derives from the fact that its base is the entire stock of government debt that carries a fixed nominal interest rate (while the base for the inflation tax is the monetary base). But, since the mere possibility that the government may resort to surprise inflation tax leads to higher interest rates, this should not be regarded as a benefit, but rather as a cost of weak credibility, which is likely to be more important for those member states which have a high public debt and a poor inflation record (e.g. Greece). Forfeiting the ability to pursue independent monetary policy is, from this perspective, welfare improving.

At macroeconomic level a variable inflation rate keeps output continuously away from the equilibrium level and involves losses. The maintaining of a balanced situation depends on the **credibility** of the monetary authority. Also, there is evidence that higher inflation and higher variability of inflation lead to higher variability in relative prices which, not being justified by changes in supply and demand conditions, cause welfare losses similar to those caused by the excessive variability of exchange-rates (Commission of the EC, 1990).

The major gain induced by the introduction of a single currency relates to the disciplinary effects it is likely to have on economic policy makers, with the subsequent benefits for the participating economies (Gerlach, 1995). Though, as Hugues Hallett and Vines (1993) warn, while viewed from within a purely European context, the strict *relative* price discipline would make monetary union appear very attractive, the lack of absolute price discipline in relation to the rest of the world will make these benefits much less certain.

4.3. EUROLAND: THE WHOLE PICTURE

The analysis of the costs and benefits associated with the introduction of a single currency in EU15 indicates clearly that these are not likely to be evenly distributed among the member states[19].

Due to the heterogeneity of EU15 member states in terms of economic structure, income per capita, unemployment etc., the economic arguments for and against the participation in EMU for each member state cannot be assessed in a revealing way on the basis of the aggregate balance of costs and benefits. In this respect, more suitable would be an estimation of their distribution across the member states.

Ideally, the case for or against the introduction of a single currency in Europe would be made on the basis of some clear monetary value resulting from a comprehensive cost-benefit analysis of the regime change. However, such an analysis is an extremely complex task and it is not definite that its outcome would be an accurate one, for a series of reasons. Firstly, it is not certain that *all* the relevant costs and benefits can be identified *a priori*. Secondly, those costs and benefits already pointed out in both theoretical and empirical literature are not always quantifiable (*a priori* or at all), reflecting most of the time qualitative aspects (e.g. loss of sovereignty). Finally, for those costs and benefits for which a quantitative expression is possible, data is not always available (at all, in a comparable form or for a long enough period of time) for all the member states, so as to enable a meaningful analysis.

We attempt minimising the impact of such limitations on the outcome of the analysis by the use of FA as a way of measuring the costs and benefits for each member state from various types of data available at country level[20].

We identify a number of empirical measures for each of the following cost-relevant country characteristics put forward in the OCA literature: magnitude and nature of nationally differentiated shocks (Bayoumi and Eichengreen, 1994a; 1994b); labour and capital mobility (Mundell, 1961; Fleming, 1971; Tower and Willett, 1976; Eichengreen, 1993); similarity of inflation rates (Fleming, 1971); openness and size of the economy (McKinnon, 1963, 1973); industrial diversification and goods markets integration (Masson and Taylor, 1993); price and wage flexibility (Fleming, 1971; Tower and Willett, 1976); fiscal integration (Masson and Taylor, 1993); long-run Phillips curve (Tavlas, 1993). To these we add empirical measures of the costs related to the loss of seigniorage revenue (Hansen, Heinrich and Nielsen, 1992; Sibert, 1994), as well as the technical costs related to the introduction of the single currency (Banking Federation of the European Union, 1995).

As far as the benefits from the single currency are concerned, the relevant ones identified in the literature - mostly produced by or under the auspices of the Commission of the EC - and included in our analysis relate to: risk elimination (Commission of the EC, 1990); elimination of transaction costs (Commission of the EC, 1990); elimination of information cost and price discrimination (Gros and Thygesen, 1992); dynamic efficiency gains (Commission of the EC, 1990; Gros and Thygesen, 1992); savings through lower official international reserves (Gross and Thygesen, 1992).

Each of these elements can be quantified in more than one way, as the literature surveyed so far indicates. The various empirical measurements on these two sets of variables are used in two successive rounds of FA. The first round of factor extraction is mainly concerned with data reduction: one single measurement is obtained for each of the relevant elements identified. The details are reported in the Factors Appendix. From the factors extracted we retain for further investigation a subset, with the statistical properties reported in part A of Table 4.1.

The next step consists in bringing all this information into a two-dimensional space, easier to perceive and interpret, by applying once more factor extraction: one for costs and one for benefits. Thus, from the previously identified unique measures for the relevant country characteristics we obtain one unique measure capturing all the cost elements and one unique measure for all the benefit elements. This is valid since the factors reported in Table 4.1 (part A) originate in different FAs and therefore are not orthogonal to each other. The outcome of the second round of factor extraction is reported in part B of the table.

Table 4.1: Costs and Benefits –Tests of Significance

	Factor	Bartlett test[a]	KMO	% of total variance explained
part A				
F34	Nationally differentiated shocks (speed of adjustment to supply disturbances)	87.64034 (.00000)	.44821	42.3
F36	Similarity of inflation rates	184.68121 (.00000)	.50000	99.3
F37	Openness and size of the economy	70.50738 (.00000)	.51449	51.7
F39	Capital mobility	.76455 (.83793)	.53110	43.9
F40	Money as symbol of national identity	2.37795 (.12306)	.50000	70.8
F30	Fiscal policy	6.29778 (.09799)	.51989	47.0

	Factor	Bartlett test[a]	KMO	% of total variance explained
F44	Labour mobility	200.68479 (.00000)	.51837	62.9
F41	Industrial diversification and goods market integration	5.87931 (.11763)	.30921	45.9
F43	Wage flexibility	5.58509 (.13364)	.39513	51.8
F46	Loss of seigniorage revenue	.70722 (.40037)	.50000	34.8
F47	Risk elimination	8.73363 (.03305)	.35795	69.1
F48	Elimination of transaction costs	46.60981 (.00000)	.66647	55.6
F49	Elimination of information costs and price discrimination	8.54901 (.3593)	.44214	59.4
F18	Dynamic efficiency gains	31.91763 (.27788)	.61817	47.8
F50	Lower official international reserves	10.93898 (.01206)	.48640	60.7
F31	Price stability	10.93260 (.09048)	.73298	62.9
part B				
FC	Costs	489.14282 (.0000)	.59203	46.7
FC*	Costs*	405.65871 (.0000)	.66830	49.4
FB	Benefits	41.20694 (.00030)	.55732	45.8

a - significance levels in parentheses

While this second round of FA is achieved at the cost of losing some more information, note that the two final factors still can explain around 50% of the variance. The F-values for the Bartlett test of sphericity allow for the rejection of the hypothesis that the population correlation matrix is an identity. This, as well as the KMO measure, indicates that the use of FA is suitable.

In order to perform a sensitivity analysis, we identify another cost factor (FC*) from which we exclude the results reported by Bayoumi and Eichengreen (1994a), contained in F34. From the statistics reported one can see that the performance is marginally improved, with the factor having a higher KMO statistic and explaining a larger share of the total variance. In the remaining analysis we do, however, continue with FC, which comprises an often cited measure of asymmetric shocks, given the importance attached to them in the literature.

From the estimated loadings reported in Table 4.2 it appears that the costs factor (FC) illustrates a tradeoff between the factors reflecting the likelihood of an asymmetric shock and the factors reflecting the ability to adjust to such a shock.

Thus, a country with high inflation (F36), low wage flexibility (F43), which relies heavily on seigniorage revenue (F46), borrows a lot from abroad (F39) and where people regard money as a symbol of national identity (F40) is more likely to face a high cost from joining the single currency.

Meanwhile, high labour mobility (F44) is predicted by the OCA literature, expected to reduce the costs incurred (it is negatively related to the costs measure, FC). Note also the minus on speed of adjustment (F34), consistent with the idea that countries with high speed of adjustment are prone to lower costs.

On the benefits side (FB), a country in need of good growth performance (F18), high level of trade with the other members (F48) and holding large official international reserves (F50) can expect larger benefits. The benefits are likely to be lower for those countries having a high level of price instability (F31) and low elasticity of demand (F49).

Table 4.2: Costs and Benefits – Structure

COSTS (FC)		BENEFITS (FB)	
variable	loading	variable	loading
F36	.93643	F49	.89735
F43	.87149	F18	-.74054
F46	.85911	F48	.71858
F40	.83737	F31	.58599
F39	.81636	F50	-.52742
F44	-.52085	F47	-.50839
F34	-.51186		
F30	.50356		
F37	-.36191		
F41	-.08286		

On the basis of the factor loadings reported in Table 4.2, factor scores are computed for each member state (as an index, with the country values of each factor weighted by the estimated loadings) with the results reported in Table 4.3.

Note that these values have no monetary significance attached; they merely measure the position of each member state relative to the European average (recall that the data has been standardised with mean zero and unit standard deviation and subsequently underwent a series of mean preserving transformations). The scores give the coordinates for a scatter plot with benefits on the horizontal axis and costs on the vertical axis (Figure 4.1), which illustrates the likely outcome of the move to the single currency in terms of the spatial distribution of the anticipated costs and benefits.

Note that Germany, on the relative gainers side, and Spain, Portugal and Greece on the relative losers side (i.e. below and respectively above the 45° line) are outstanding cases. Note also that most member states are clustered around the origin, close to the 45° line, indicating an almost balanced outcome, with small relative net gains for most of the member states. Among the countries traditionally considered as belonging to the core, Italy is likely to be on the losers side, while the Benelux, France and UK could expect some gains. The same is true for Denmark (and less so for the other Northern members, who are much closer to the 45° line) and for Austria.

These results are very much in line with the 'late two-speed EMU' scenario put forward by Eichengreen and Frieden (1993) and even more so with the findings of Bayoumi and Eichengreen (1997), based on an OCA index constructed (through regression analysis) on the basis of several proxies for output disturbance, trade linkages and usefulness of money for transactions.

Table 4.3: Spatial Distribution of Costs and Benefits

Country	Costs score	Benefits score
Austria	-1.13696	-0.62150
Belgium	-2.19283	-0.04536
Denmark	-0.66734	0.72885
Finland	-0.53784	0.78272
France	-0.64067	0.70018
Germany	-1.78259	3.90519
Greece	4.24252	-3.53681
Ireland	-0.86166	-0.65218
Italy	0.72460	-0.03657
Luxembourg	-.075181	0.6499
Netherlands	-2.39125	0.09752
Portugal	3.54476	-3.83269
Spain	2.05402	-1.15246
Sweden	0.47604	1.42049
UK	-0.07627	2.17764

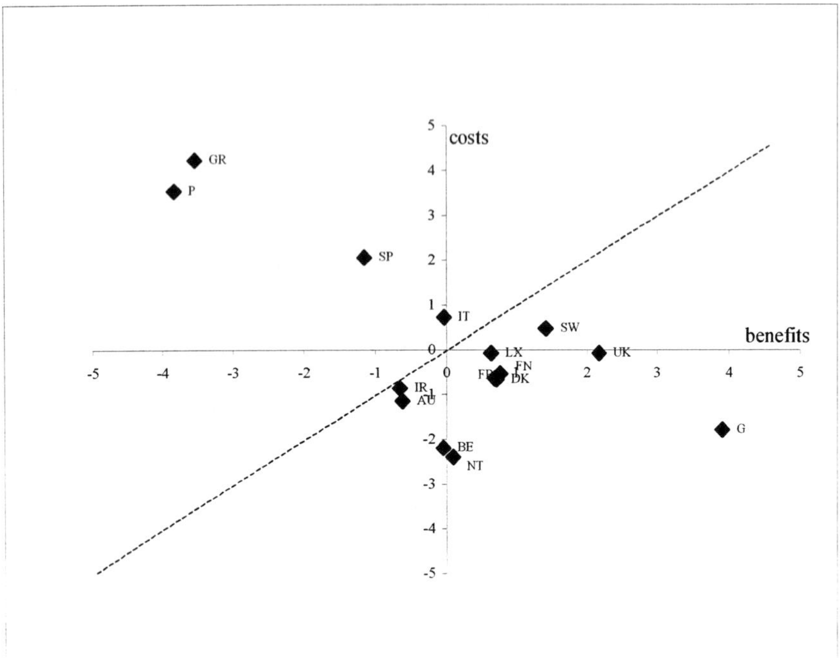

Figure 4.1: Relative costs and benefits

The absence of a significance test makes it impossible to assess what distance from the 45° line, on either side, should be regarded as substantial. However, we can further investigate what is it that actually makes a member state a potential gainer or a potential loser. This is relevant in terms of policy implications, in that countries could enhance their characteristics closely related to an increased likelihood of gaining. This could also be reinforced with some policy measures at European level.

DA enables us to determine statistically, by an analysis of variance, those linear combinations of country characteristics that best discriminate between potential losers and gainers from the introduction of the single currency (see Technical Appendix for mathematical details). We can thus identify, among the elements prescribed by the OCA literature, the ones that, in the case of the EU, are most important in separating potential gainers from potential losers, with the following results:

Table 4.4: Gainers vs. Losers, Members vs. Non-Members of the Euro-Zone

variable	standardised canonical discriminant function coefficients	
	A	B
F34	-0.91591	3.055

F36	-0.49247	6.247
F37	2.56076	-0.021
F39	-0.16388	-14.514
F40	3.21319	15.471
F41	-1.86208	-1.831
F43	-1.23043	0.283
F44	-1.29822	5.733
F46	-2.33105	
F47		-1.502
F48	1.13522	1.331
F49	0.14798	7.161
F18	3.65316	
F30	-0.29108	2.768
eigenvalue	63.17	25.866
Wilks' lambda[a] [chi-square]	27.050 (.0122)	23.036 (.027)

a - significance levels in parentheses

On the basis of the estimated parameters of the discriminant functions (interpreted like in multiple regression analysis) we infer that the most important elements within the OCA framework in discriminating between potential losers and gainers are, in decreasing order of the absolute value of the estimated parameters (column A): dynamic efficiency gains (F18), regarding money as a symbol of national identity (F40), openness and size of the economy (F37) and seigniorage revenue (F46).

Therefore one could argue that the most developed and faster growing countries, who attach less importance to the loss of the national currency as a symbolic loss of sovereignty, those countries that are more open to trade with the other member states, while displaying low levels of inflation (relying less on seigniorage revenue), are more likely to gain from the move to the single currency. This clarifies the position on the map occupied by Germany, which may seem counterintuitive to some: this is the country closest to the average EU image in relationship to which the positions are measured.

As for the actual membership of the euro-zone (column B), the dominant characteristics that distinguish between members and nonmembers, as identified by DA, are: regarding money as symbol of national identity (F40), followed by capital mobility (F39), information costs and price discrimination (F49) and inflation rates (F36). Note that none of these factors have been central to the OCA analysis, in the way labour mobility and wage flexibility have.

As far as the statistical properties of the DA functions estimated are concerned, note that both have large eigenvalues (i.e. large ratios of the between-groups to within-groups sums of squares) which, according to Norušis (1994), are associated with 'good' functions (p.16). Note also that the eigenvalue is much higher for the first function, the one separating relative losers from relative gainers.

The significance of the estimated functions is also reflected in the estimated Wilks' lambda parameters. The large corresponding chi-square values (very low p-values) enable us to reject the null hypothesis that potential relative losers and potential relative gainers (respectively members and nonmembers) have the same means on the discriminant function.

It is clear from this analysis that not all the EU member-states can be expected to perform close to the European average, following the introduction of the single currency. More specifically, some can expect a relative net gain from abandoning independent monetary policy-making, some others can anticipate a relative net loss.

Since, at least in the short and medium run, not all the EU15 member states are likely to gain from the introduction of the single currency, one wonders about their motivation in deciding to move to the EMU.

According to De Grauwe (1993), monetary union has been regarded by many actual or potential member states as a means of solving the credibility problem of their national monetary policies. The main argument is that when the government can make a binding pre-commitment to an *ex ante* optimal policy, in the presence of an imperfection (an externality, a market distortion or a lack of policy instrument) there will be no longer an *ex post* incentive to deviate from the first best outcome. Since reputation may be a complete or partial substitute for formal pre-commitments, and thus lower or eliminate the costs of the credibility problem (Persson, 1988), by giving up its independent monetary policy and entering a MU with a low-inflation country, a high-inflation country can, under the rational expectations assumption, increase its credibility and reduce the costs induced by surprise (dis)inflation.

It follows that, as Backus and Driffill (1985) argue, a finite-horizon government concerned with inflation and employment has the possibility of credibly avoiding an excessive inflation rate for some time by mimicking the policy of a hard-nosed government, i.e. a government concerned only with inflation.

Using the Barro-Gordon (1983) model of two countries it can be shown that, when the common inflation rate is identical (or close) to the one in the low-inflation country, all the gains are for the high-inflation countries (De Grauwe, 1994a). In a system accepting the leadership of the low-inflation country, the high-inflation country maximises its welfare without reducing the welfare of the low-inflation country. Therefore, for countries such as Italy and Spain, EMU is likely to yield a more stable low-inflation environment. As for Germany, such an arrangement will yield at maximum no gains, when the common inflation rate is identical to its inflation rate, or a welfare loss when the common inflation rate is higher than its own.

The key factor becomes the credibility of the ECB, whose commitment cannot be based on its own history of low inflation and independence from short-term political pressures (like in the case of the Bundesbank), but depends on the nature of the institutional arrangements on which its creation relies (Corden, 1994).

This could help rationalise a German interest in keeping the size of EMU small, since a currency union with few members will allow Germany to minimise its welfare loss, while preserving its dominant position in the monetary policy-making in Europe. Actually De Grauwe (1993) argues that the convergence criteria imposed by the Maastricht Treaty are not based on sound economic reasons but express the German interest in keeping the size of the union small.

For other countries, like France, the participation in EMU is equivalent to a guarantee for the increase in their influence on monetary affairs at European level. Besides this politically attractive idea, the acceptance of the tight nominal convergence requirements imposed by Maastricht was for most member states both a way to show their commitment to the goal of MU and an expression of their confidence that they can 'beat the Germans at their own game' (De Grauwe, 1993).

It follows that, from the perspective of the political economy arguments, the final outcome does not depend much on whether Europe is an OCA or not. The main factor appears to be the political will, as it was the case in the recent German unification. An example "in reverse" is the one of the former Soviet Union, for which OCA arguments failed to explain the collapse of the Rouble area.

As Bayoumi, Eichengreen and von Hagen (1997) argue, 'the literature which adopts a narrowly economic approach provides only limited insight into the likely outcome of the EMU project. It is on political economy rather than narrowly economic grounds that the battle over EMU has and will be fought' (p.71).

The findings reported so far suggest that the introduction of a single currency is likely to 'split' Europe into gainers and losers. We turn next to the implication of these results for the envisaged enlargement towards Central and Eastern Europe.

NOTES

[1] See Vaubel (1990) for an alternative based on currency competition as a means of determining the optimal number and pattern of currency domains and a parallel currency as a second best solution.

[2] An OCA is usually defined as a group of economic entities (individuals, regions or countries) among which welfare is maximised through fixed internal rates or a common currency, and a flexible exchange rate towards the rest of the world. See Beine, Candelon and Hecq (2000) for a narrower definition.

[3] For surveys see: Ishiyama (1973); Tower and Willett (1976); Tavlas (1993).

[4] The limited attention paid to the benefits is due, according to Viñals (1996) to the theoretical difficulties in modeling the role of money, which preclude the identification of the structure of transaction costs and thus the quantification of the benefits of eliminating them.

[5] See Viñals (1996) for a discussion of the difficulties related to providing empirical evidence on the costs and benefits of EMU. See also Eichengreen and Ghironi (1995); see McKibbin and Bok (1994) for an attempt to 'measure' the costs in terms of the implications for the variance of key variables in the face of a variety of shocks, under alternative regimes.

[6] As pointed out by Corden (1994), when policy tastes differ, MU imposes a cost even if shocks (resulting from a union-wide terms-of-trade deterioration or a recession) are symmetric.

[7] However, his theory is open to criticism on the grounds that the direction of factor flows is ambiguous: while capital may flow more to the dynamic regions, labour may be relatively immobile and reluctant to move from the depressed regions (Harrop, 1992); moreover, high skilled and younger workers are more likely to be mobile.

[8] This happens because factor input ratios are similar in both the export and the import substitute sectors, and relative factor prices do not therefore have to alter to the same extent to maintain full employment (Krugman, 1981).

[9] For an overview of the migration policy within the member states see Commission of the EC (1985). See also Rudden and Wyatt (1994).

[10] See Hofstede (1990) for cultural barriers and Molle and Van Mourik (1988) for an outline of the dynamics of labour migration in EC6, EC9 and EC12.

[11] This is in the sense that they cannot influence the world price of the goods they trade.

[12] See Masson and Taylor, (1993); Sala-i-Martin and Sachs (1992); Genberg and Nadal de Simone (1993). Also, see McKinnon (1994) for a disagreeing view.

[13] Sibert (1994) shows that in a currency area, the coexistence of independent fiscal policy makers and a common independent central bank which can choose the allocation of seigniorage will lead to higher than optimal inflation and lower than optimal government spending and taxes. The recommended solution for avoiding the non-optimal outcome is by limiting the central bank's ability to follow discretionary policy.

[14] Data come from Flash Eurobarometer (1995) and Europinion (1996).

[15] For surveys on the empirical literature see Commission of the EC (1990), Gros and Thygesen (1992), and Abbott (2001).

[16] Things are further complicated by the fact that not all 15 EU member states are part of the EMU, creating the need for an exchange rate between outsiders and insiders.

[17] McKinnon (1994) estimates the money changing costs incurred by tourists at over 5% of the gross transaction value, while business firms are faced with a cost of less than 1/4% of the gross value of the transactions. See also Gros and Thygesen, (1990).

[18] The outcome depends on the sources of inflation, on its anticipated or unanticipated nature, on the institutional structure of the economy, on the fact that the inflation rate is not an exogenous variable to the economy (Fischer, 1981).

[19] They are not likely to be evenly distributed across interest groups in different countries either; see Eichengreen and Frieden (1993) for a discussion along these lines.

[20] This analysis is largely based on our previous work on the single currency in Porojan (2001).

Chapter 5

ENLARGEMENT

5.1. HISTORY AND THEORY

There is virtually no literature on the 'economics of enlargement' as such. However, one might consider relevant here the vast literature on regional integration, mainly the part related to the economic rationale of forming free trade areas (FTAs) and customs unions (CUs) pioneered by Viner (1950)[1].

In the case of the EU enlargement towards CEECs, integration is to take place between two distinct groups of countries: the advanced, relatively industrial Western Europe and the less developed, relatively agriculture-oriented Eastern Europe. Brada and Mendez (1993) argue that a CU formed between an agrarian and an industrialised country 'will only serve to capture the markets of one partner for the other at the expense of third countries, thus largely diverting trade'[2] (p.185). Meanwhile, integrating competitive economies (i.e. economies producing similar products at divergent unit costs) will lead to more trade creation. Thus, in terms of the Vinerian analysis (i.e. trade creation *vs.* trade diversion) the enlargement of the EU towards CEE does not provide a strong economic rationale, since instead of significant welfare gains from trade creation, the participating countries are likely to be faced with trade diversion.

Brada and Mendez (1993) also point out that small countries might be interested in joining with a larger partner in order to achieve a larger market for their industries and thus reap a disproportionate share of the gains from integration. Spilimbergo and Stein (1996) show that, under the presence of similar tariff levels across the countries involved, poor countries will always prefer to integrate with rich countries, due to both product variety and comparative advantage considerations[3]. To these elements of 'new regionalism', Srinivasan, Whalley and Wooton (1993) add the search for "safe-haven trade agreements" by smaller countries motivated by the desire to secure access to the markets of large neighbouring trading partners because of fears of higher trade barriers in the future (i.e. the insurance value of secure access to a large market), and the desire of developing countries to lock in domestic policy reforms by signing regional arrangements (easier to negotiate than multilateral ones). Meanwhile, the large country would expect only limited economic benefits (Brada and Mendez, 1993; Baldwin, Francois and Portes, 1997).

In the EU-CEECs scenario, this could mean that the CEECs are individually (i.e. as small countries) more motivated to join the EU than the EU itself or the CEECs as a bloc.

Two are the main forces driving enlargement: political considerations and expected economic gains. As far as the incumbents are concerned, the political motivation might be strong enough to more than compensate for the lack of economic incentives on the EU side. As Baldwin (1995) points out, the strongest force behind the EU's decision to enlarge eastward is the one of 'high politics'. The estimated net cost of the Eastern enlargement on the EU15 is around 0.01% of the GDP of EU15, or ECU 8 bn, according to Baldwin, Francois and Portes (1997) who argue that '[T]his is an extraordinarily low cost given the historic challenge in Central Europe. Imagine how eager western Europe would have been in the 1980s to pay ECU 8 billion a year in order to free central Europe from communism and remove Soviet troops from the region' (p.168). Still, some do perceive the accession of these candidates as threatening (Inotai, 2000).

In Mansfield's (1993) view, there is a clear tendency for regional integration agreements to form and evolve among allies[4], since alliances help to internalise the security externalities generated by trade, and to increase the reliability of access to the markets of trading partners.

Meanwhile, in the Johnsonian approach (see Johnson, 1965; Brada and Mendez, 1993), small, relatively less-developed countries are likely to form customs unions for the sake of fulfilling common objectives. This points towards the suitability of a CEE bloc, of the Central European Free-Trade Area (CEFTA) type, set up by the Visegrad group. Yet, in our view, this is so much reminiscent of the old Council for Mutual Economic Assistance (CMEA) that it remains rejected on political grounds, despite the economic rationale[5]. Instead, EU membership carries a symbolic value, being regarded as acknowledgement from the West of their departure from communism. As Baldwin (1995) puts it, '[F]or the Central European countries, EU membership would symbolically restore them to their historical position among the advanced industrial economies of continental Europe. More importantly, membership would have a decisive impact on the domestic political scenes of all CEECs by firmly closing the book on authoritarianism - just as it did in Greece, Portugal and Spain' (p.480).

This comes to confirm the remark of Brada and Mendez (1993) concerning the limited relevance of economic factors to the formation of regional integration schemes. In this specific case, political and economic arguments appear to compete each other rather than complement each other. To quote Baldwin, Francois and Portes (1997), geopolitical considerations constitute the engine driving enlargement, while the economic and financial considerations act as the brake.

An interesting view on enlargement is offered by the 'domino theory of regionalism' put forward by Baldwin (1993b). Deeper integration of a regional bloc, he argues, is detrimental to the profit of firms in non-member countries and thus stimulates them to engage in greater pro-membership political activity. This extra activity may tilt the balance towards membership, in the case of a government previously close to indifference to membership. When the bloc enlarges, the cost to non-members increases and the domino effect continues. There is in this argument an implicit positive relationship between 'deeper' and 'wider' regional integration, which runs against our findings. In our opinion this related essentially to the fact that Baldwin (1993b) did not model the supply side of membership, i.e. did not question whether the incumbents would welcome the new entrants.

Another stream of literature takes into account the intrinsic characteristics of the participating countries and has as focal point the likelihood and implications of a multi-speed evolution of the European integration process (e.g., Alesina and Grilli, 1993; Viñals, 1996; De Grauwe 1994a, 1994b). In this context, dissimilarities and divergent tendencies across the member states have a major impact on the achievement of the EU objectives. To quote Britton and Mayes (1990), '[T]he formation of EMU is itself [...] a powerful force for convergence, but the "glue" of monetary union will not be powerful enough to hold the component parts together if their inherent tendency to spring apart is still too strong' (p.953).

Understanding the enlargement objective requires, as Baldwin (1995) prompts, taking into account what influences both the entrants and the incumbents in taking such a step: economics (i.e. standard aggregate welfare gain or loss), 'low' politics (i.e. interest groups' reactions) and 'high' politics (i.e. the role of European integration in maintaining peace and democracy).

Such an approach is however beyond the scope of our research. Instead, our aim is to build around another remark of Baldwin (1995), namely that the CEEC economies are *very different* to the average EU economy. We use as starting point the arguments developed by Alesina and Grilli (1993). Starting from a loss function focused on the trade-off between the average inflation and the variance of output, they explore the feasibility of a one-speed or multi-speed EMU and find that whereas 'one-speed' union would be feasible (in the sense that all participating countries would not be worse off with the union than without the union), a multi-speed process would stop the union at a smaller group of countries. Furthermore, they argue that in the presence of two clusters of countries very similar to each other within each group but with sizeable differences across groups, that it is very likely that a two-speed Europe will never lead to a complete Europe, and the creation of 'two monetary unions' might result. The reason behind the outcome is the opposition of the 'incumbents' to accept new members with very different preferences from the 'median union member', since the loss due to the change in the political equilibrium of the enlarged union could more than offset the benefits of the new entry.

With respect to the enlargement towards CEE, a similar implication can be found in the idea put forward by Bofinger (1995): given the fact that participation in the EU's distributional schemes is a clear case of zero-sum game, with the incumbents losing what the new members gain, the inclusion of the CEECs one by one will increase the number of poor incumbents and make the "lobby of the poor" oppose the accession of other low income countries[6] and transform the EU more and more into a "closed shop". Obviously, this holds true as long as the rules of the distribution stay unchanged.

An even more dramatic outcome is anticipated by Agnew (2001), who argues that the goal of a single Europe is, in the context of increased inequality, tuning into 'a vision of multiple Europes' (p.36) supporting the global competitiveness of the EU as a whole.

5.2. Multi-Tier Structure in Europe

The idea of multi-tier structure is relevant both at the EU15 level and in a hypothetical, enlarged union, where the potential members are taken into account.

Before exploring the degree of similarity between existing and potential members, we use CA in order to identify relatively homogenous groups of countries within EU15, using as variables the set of factors extracted in the previous chapter. The relevant details can be found in the Technical Appendix.

The dendogram in Figure 5.1 summarises the clustering process. Our attention is drawn to the three-clusters solution (vertical cut between 10 and 19) which delivers a quasi-geographic outcome: the Northern members cluster together, and so do the 'core' countries and, respectively, the Southern member states. Note also that there is a persistent divide between Spain, Portugal and Greece, on the one hand, and the rest of EU15 on the other hand (vertical cut beyond 5).

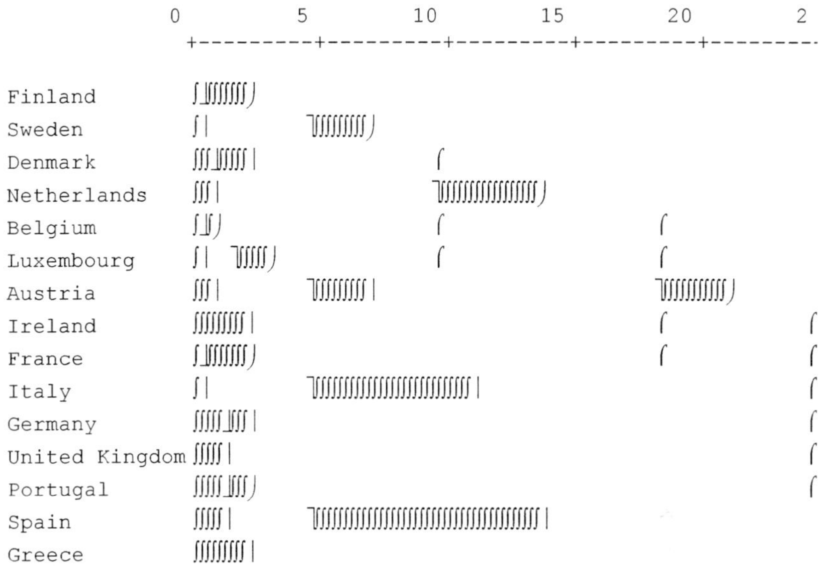

Figure 5.1: Cluster membership: EU15

It is important to identify those characteristics that have a major contribution to separating the 'core' from 'periphery', the Northern from the Southern states. We further investigate the three-clusters solution through DA. The estimated functions have the properties reported below.

The estimated coefficients for the first function suggest that expectations about the national economy (F5), sustainable growth (F18) and the sense of national integration (F15) are the crucial variables distinguishing between the various tiers of EU members. To these, the second function adds intra-EU trade (F11) and employment (F14). Meanwhile, expectations about Europe (F7), government intervention (F3) and the standard of living (F12) contribute to a diminished divergence among the member states[7].

Next, we investigate the profile of an enlarged union. We now use CA to explore whether the EU members, on the one hand, and the potential members, on the other hand, do belong to different groups, not on the basis of membership to certain institutional arrangements, but on the basis of their intrinsic characteristics (economic, political, social and cultural).

The 38 countries have been classified on the basis of the information contained in 41 economic indicators[8], with the outcome depicted in Figure 5.2 (a and b).

Table 5.1: Core vs. Periphery in EU15

Variable (Factor)	Standardised canonical discriminant function coefficients	
	Function 1	Function 2
F1	-1.73544	-0.52624
F3	-5.74671	-2.17856
F5	22.96037	7.07650
F7	-23.99739	1.25487
F9	2.67556	-0.84722
F11	2.42073	11.29412
F12	-3.42664	-2.94954
F14	-0.91525	5.43732
F17	0.02606	0.54719
F15	3.04775	6.97832
F18	6.99892	-5.08532
F25	-0.56916	-1.99798
canonical correlation	0.9984	0.9948
% of total variance explained	76.44	23.56
eigenvalue	310.397	95.6858
Wilks' lambda[a] [chi-square]	67.031 (.0000)	29.715 (.0018)

a - levels of significance in parentheses

The most informative appears to be the solutions with three and four clusters: while they offer more information than the two cluster solution, in terms of illustrating the differences across the countries analysed, they are not too difficult to follow (as the solutions with larger numbers of clusters usually are).

The EU members appear to belong to three groups, with Greece and Portugal in one group, France, Germany and UK plus Italy and Spain in one group, and Austria, Belgium, Denmark, Finland, Ireland, Luxembourg, Netherlands and Sweden in another. Note the similarity to the outcome in the previous section, which would indicate the predominance of economic factors in discriminating between the various groups.

As far as the potential members are concerned, Poland, Ukraine, Turkey and Russia belong to the 'large country group'; Cyprus clusters with Greece and Portugal, while the remaining potential members form a group of their own.

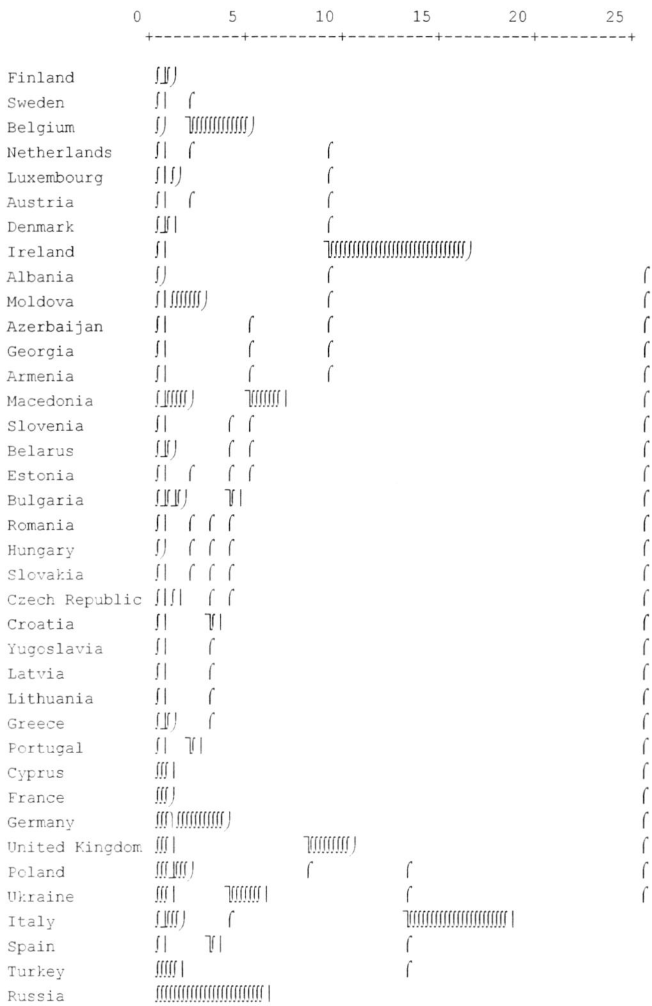

Figure 5.2a: Cluster membership: enlarged EU (economic characteristics)

The dendogram in Figure 5.2b presents the results obtained when Russia, 'the limit case' (Economist, 1999) is excluded from the sample. Note the consistency of the results obtained in the two specifications.

The same countries have been grouped on the basis of seven political variables[9], with the results reported in Figure 5.3 (a and b).

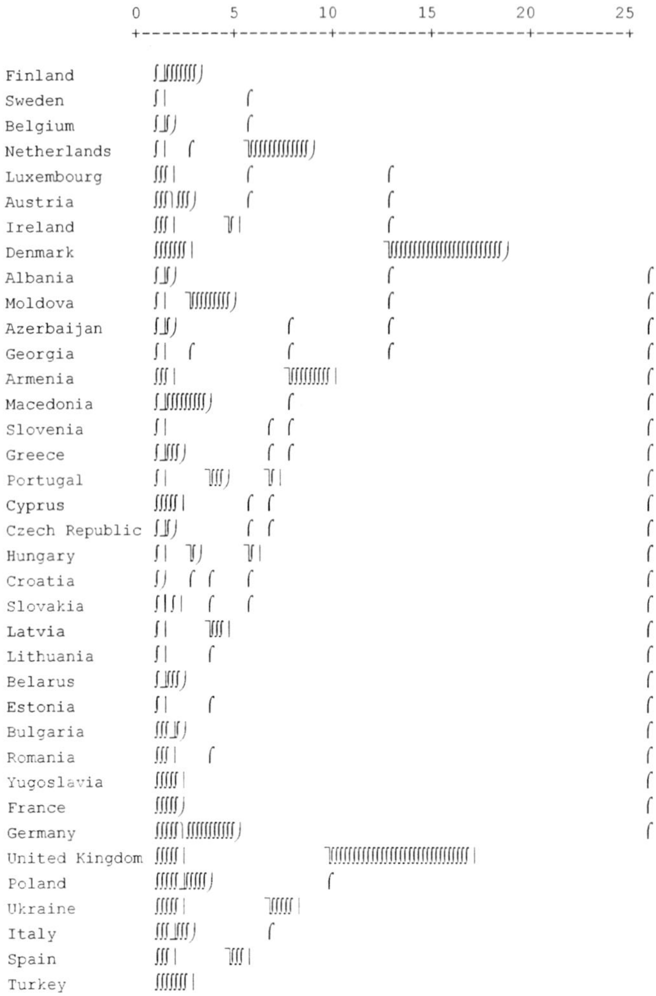

Figure 5.2b: Cluster membership: enlarged EU (economic characteristics) - Russia not included

One has to regard these findings with caution, since the selection of the variables included was restricted by the data availability for all the countries in the sample; the missing cases have been replaced by the sample mean, introducing thus a bias towards more homogenous groups than otherwise.

At the four-clusters solution the EU member states belong three distinct groups, but with different composition from the ones defined by the measures on economic characteristics. Note the isolated group formed by the core members (France, Italy, Germany, UK), clearly distinct from the other EU15 countries and from all potential members.

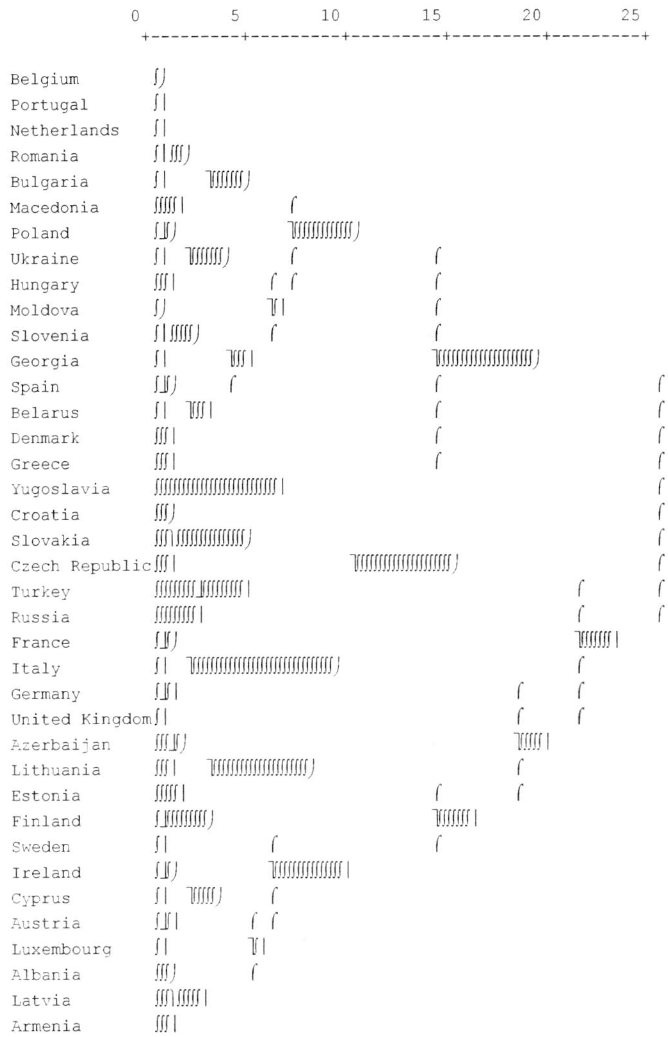

Figure 5.3a: Cluster membership: enlarged EU (political characteristics)

For consistency, Figure 5.3b reports the results obtained when Russia is excluded from the sample.

When grouping the countries in the sample on the basis of 25 social and cultural indicators[10], the results reported in Figure 5.4 (a and b) have been obtained.

At the four-cluster solution (vertical cut between 6 and 8), the existing EU15 fall into two groups: the ‘poor’ Greece, Spain, Ireland and Portugal in one group, and the ‘rich’ remaining members in another.

As far as the potential members are concerned, Cyprus joins the ‘poor’ EU15 members’ group, Turkey groups with Albania and Macedonia, and

Russia with the rest of the CEECs. When Russia is not in the sample (Figure 5.4b), the results change slightly, in that Turkey stands alone, while Albania and Macedonia joint the other CEECs.

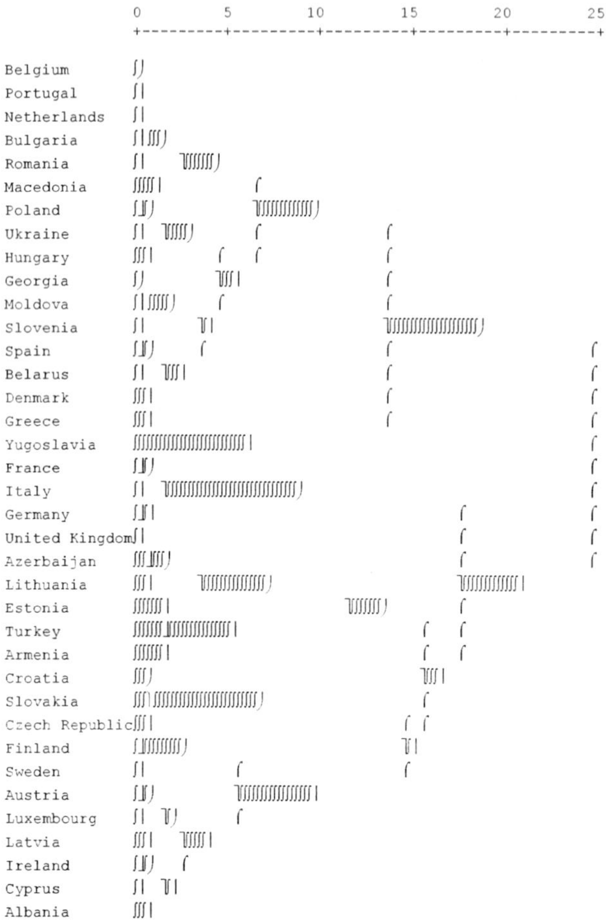

Figure 5.3b: Cluster membership: enlarged EU (political characteristics) - Russia not included

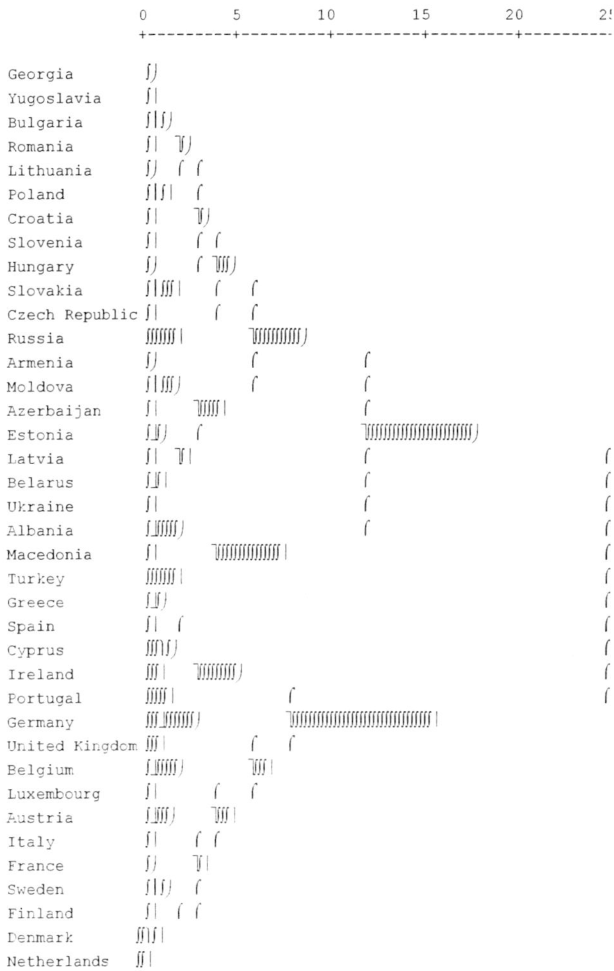

Figure 5.4a: Cluster membership: enlarged EU (social and cultural characteristics)

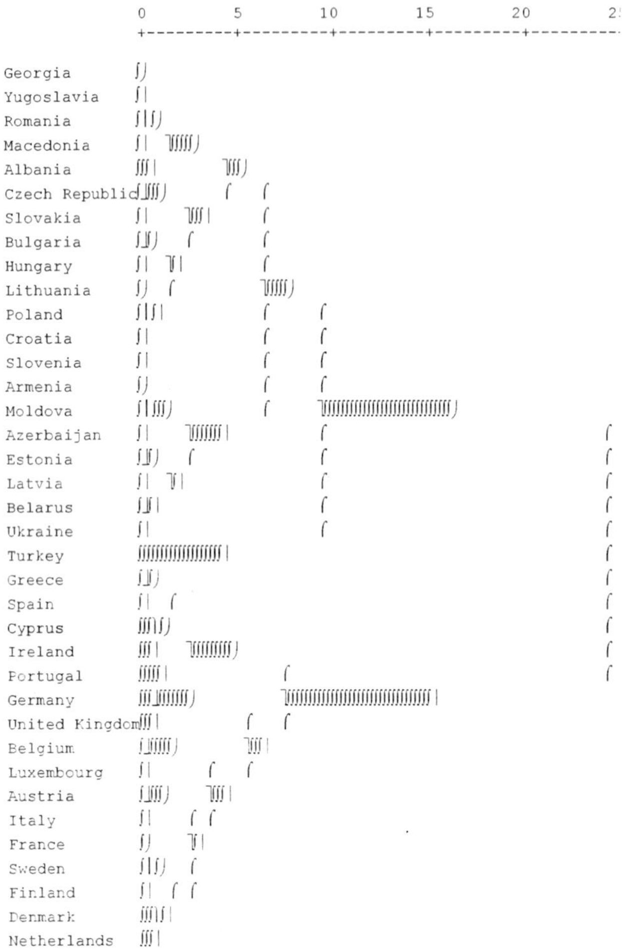

Figure 5.4b: Cluster membership: enlarged EU (social and cultural characteristics) - Russia not included

5.3. Two vs. Three Speed Europe

Although our approach departs from the traditional hypothesis testing procedure, being mainly an application of multivariate statistical exploratory techniques, our results can be interpreted along the lines of Alesina and Grilli (1993).

There is some evidence of a multi-tier structure of the EU15. This makes the success of a 15 member states EMU questionable. The current Euroland11 has the potential for becoming an 'elite' EMU, including the core countries, and risks making the possibility of all the 15 member states having the same currency remote, unless the countries left out at the first stage agree to change their preferences. Moreover, the possibility of an EU enlargement towards CEE appears thus even more far-off, since, given the existing relative internal homogeneity of the CEECs and distinctiveness from EU15, it can be expected to add a third tier to the two-tier (core *vs.* periphery) EU. This lends some support to the pessimistic views expressed by Agnew (2001) and Smith (2002).

At this stage we have no statistical means for testing the significance of the degree of similarity among the countries belonging to a cluster in connection to the degree of dissimilarity across clusters in the spirit of Alesina and Grilli (1993). Instead, we turn to looking into the relevance of our findings in terms of policy implications at both national and European level.

NOTES

[1] See Srinivasan, Whalley and Wooton (1993) for a comprehensive survey of the theoretical and empirical literature on the issue. See also, among others: Brada and Mendez (1985); Winters (1985); Frankel, Stein and Wei (1993); Krugman (1991); Baldwin, Francois and Portes (1997).

[2] *Trade diversion* refers to the shift in imports from the least cost exporter to the more expensive product from the partner countries in a regional integration agreement. *Trade creation* refers to the substitution of imports of lower-cost goods produced by a country's partner for its own domestic products and thus reflects the trade expansion between partner countries in accordance with international comparative advantage.

[3] In the EU-CEECs scenario, the distinctions rich-poor and small-large overlap to a certain extent (i.e. if one regards the EU as a large-rich potential partner for relatively small-poor CEECs (see also Baldwin, Francois and Portes (1997) on the issue of size and for some evidence on asymmetry of protection rates).

[4] Note the 1999 accession to NATO of three of the 'first wave' candidates (Czech Republic, Hungary, Poland).

[5] The question of the existence of such an economic rationale could be further investigated, on the grounds of the findings of Spilimbergo and Stein (1996), that a poor country would consider joining another poor country (rather than a rich partner) only if the two are proximate and transportation costs are sufficiently high. See Genberg and Nadal de Simone (1993) for 'eleven additional explanations' for the relative failure of regional integration agreements among developing countries.

[6] This is very relevant since the existing poor members account for about 1/5 of the EU's population and are very close to having a blocking minority in the Council of Ministers (Bofinger, 1995).

[7] According to Norušis (1985), the signs of the coefficients are arbitrary.

[8] V2, V56, V80, V81, V82, V83, V84, V87, V89, V90, V91, V92, V93, V94, V97, V98, V99, V100, V105, V106, V107, V108, V109, V110, V114, V115, V116, V117, V118, V119, V120, V121, V122, V123, V124, V125, V126, V127, V130, V131, V135 (see the Data Appendix for definitions and sources).

[9] V38, V44, V49, V54, V59, V60, V67;

[10] V1, V5, V6, V7, V8, V9, V10, V12, V13, V14, V15, V16, V17, V19, V20, V21, V24, V29, V30, V33, V34, V35, V123, V124, V125.

Chapter 6

POLICY IMPLICATIONS

6.1. OBJECTIVES AND INSTRUMENTS

There is a substantial overlap between national and European objectives, since the member states regard the EU as a setting capable of enhancing the achievement of nationally valued goals (high standard of living, growth etc.). Thus, to a certain extent, attaining nationally set objectives would coincide with an European achievement.

From our results it can be inferred that, in order to be successful in the pursuit of sustainable growth and standard of living, the member states need to concentrate their efforts on maintaining credibility (so as to influence expectations) and promoting trade relations with each other and the rest of the world. This could be looked at in connection to the findings of Quah (1996), that, for explaining regional distribution dynamics (i.e. changes in time in spatial disparities), physical location and geographical spillovers 'matter more' than do national macro factors. If this is the case, catching up with the good performance of the 'neighbours' could find in trade an appropriate channel, given the repeatedly acknowledged relevance of the relationship between geography and trade (see, e.g., Krugman, 1991). In evaluating this choice it is worth noting that, while the empirical literature based on cross-section appears to find a close and fairly robust relationship between exports and growth, the time series results are less conclusive.

In the long run, investment in human capital emerges as a valuable option. This appears to be in line with the prescriptions of the so-called 'new growth theory', which stresses the role of investment in human capital (besides physical capital) as a driving force in the growth process, and puts emphasis on the positive externalities to investment and the spillover effects of learning (e.g., Greenaway and Sapsford, 1994).

Interestingly, the achievement of sustainable growth and high standards of living is not supported but hindered by manifestations of nationalistic attitudes. In other words, countries that place a higher value on national identity (and military expenditure) are less likely to sustain a high growth and standard of living. On the other hand, one could regard as relevant here the distinction pointed out by Lundberg (1994) between *formal* sovereignty, in the sense of legal control over policy parameters, and the *actual* ability to control such target variables, strongly related, in the case of the EU members, to the country's power to influence decision-making on a supranational level. To what extent each member state tries (and succeeds) to promote national (or even nationalistic) interests at European level remains an open question[1].

Recall the negligible weight attached to government intervention in our results in Chapter 4. This outcome could be regarded as a reflection of the fact that market integration increases the cross-border effects of macroeconomic policies, and thus macroeconomic interdependence and the need for policy integration (Genberg and Nadal de Simone, 1993). If one was to regard the government intervention factor as an indicator of the size of government, our findings would be not conclusive with respect to the negative relationship between size of government and growth in the spirit of Barro and Sala-i-Martin (1995).

It appears that at European, as well as at national level, the role of expectations is fundamental. Maintaining credibility at this level is essential and relates mainly to the success of the single market programme. Certainly, to this one needs to add the impact of all the political and economic changes in anticipation of and following the move to the single currency[2].

While our findings based on CCA can contribute to the choice, in practical terms, among goals and instruments, they must be supplemented by policy judgements meant to establish priorities among goals. This is, as Adelman, Geier and Morris (1969) argue, 'because targets which are comparatively difficult to achieve may be extremely important and thus be worth pursuit in preference to more easily attainable objectives' (p.409).

It is beyond the scope of this analysis to attempt a ranking of the various European objectives. However, it appears that some priorities ought to be defined, given the apparent negative relationship (*trade-off*) between Eastern *enlargement* and standard of living, on the one hand, and *single currency* and price stability on the other hand. These results should be regarded with caution, given the uncertainties implied by an *ex-ante* measurement of the single currency and enlargement objectives.

The trade-off between the two 'new' objectives (single currency and enlargement) is, implicitly, acknowledged by several authors. Goodhart (1991), for instance, finds in the 'desire and need' to bring the CEECs into the EU a 'reason for pause' in the rush towards the introduction of the single currency, since 'the further and faster the process towards a federal, integrated, centralised Western Europe, the more difficult it may be for the countries of Eastern Europe to join [...]' (p.17). To what extent pursuing both objectives is going to appear more costly than the pursuit of only one of the objectives remains to be seen; even when a trade-off exists between the two objectives, the possibility of issue trading (i.e. 'single currency' in exchange of 'enlargement' in the negotiation between member states with different priorities) might mitigate the overall costs.

Fiscal policy, in its current design, appears to be opposing the former couple of objectives (enlargement and standard of living), while sustaining the latter (single currency and price stability). This can be related to the findings of Hughes Hallett and Vines (1993) that, since monetary union is particularly dependent on supporting fiscal policies, the proper coordination of fiscal policies with monetary policy is essential to the success of the EMU. That is, they say, a matter of increasing the effectiveness of existing policy instruments and not of introducing a new policy regime.

Our results can also be linked to the expressed fear regarding the impact of enlargement on the budgetary arrangements: with the existing setting, the move is unappealing to both the current net contributors - reluctant to accept a further increase in their burden, and the existing net beneficiaries - likely to loose their position with the increase in the number of members qualifying for support from the European budget. Baldwin (1995) reports some estimates which speak for themselves: the admission of the Visegrad countries in the year 2000 would have increased the annual EU spending by 60% of the EU's projected budget in 2000; under the current rule that a region is eligible for the largest share of EU structural spending as long as its average income is less than 75% of the EU average, the Visegrad countries would need two decades before reaching the cut-off level (with EU average income growing at 2% and the Visegrad countries ones at 6%). The picture is even more bleak if one looks at the findings of Knell (1995) regarding the number of years necessary for the CEECs to catch up with the EU average: from a minimum of 16 years for the Czech Republic and Slovenia (with a 5% positive growth differential) to a maximum 183 years for Romania (with a 1% positive growth differential). The recent Treaty of Nice, by the far-reaching reforms of the EU that it brings, aims to alleviate the concerns of the existing member states over the limitations of the current institutional arrangements in view of enlargement. It remains to be seen whether these changes will ease the process as much as expected.

An interesting insight into the apparent trade-off between single currency and enlargement is offered by the political economy literature, centred on the role of Germany in the European integration process. It is widely agreed that Germany is not in for large economic gains with the move to the single currency[3] (Eichengreen and Ghironi, 1995). Motivating its commitment to further integration in general and the single currency in particular might rest on issue trading across policy areas. One such issue could be enlargement of the EU to encompass CEE, given that support for political and economic stability in Eastern Europe remains a higher priority for Germany than for other member states. If membership would be refused to the CEECs, they argue, Germany would 'feel obliged' to make transfers to the East on its own, having less German money to transfer to the Southern EU members (which would, in turn, increase the pressure on France to 'take up the slack'.

A more conciliatory position is taken by Wijkman (1992) who sustains that the Maastricht Treaty already contains 'important elements of variable geometry and of a multi-speed approach to common objectives', which should provide 'sufficient flexibility to allow deepening and enlargement to proceed continuously' (p.17).

While the introduction of the single currency is incompatible with the idea of national identity, the enlargement towards CEE appears as a threat to European identity, as defined by EU15.

As for the role of political authority, we find that the centralisation of the political power at the European level does not play a major role in the achievement of the common objectives. One can regard this as an indication that the current structure and functioning of the European institutions is not appropriate for the pursuit of the 'new' objectives (see the idea of institutional reform on the 1996/97 and 2000 inter-governmental conferences' agendae). This is an important aspect when read through the findings of Martin (1993), that the outcomes of the EMU process 'cannot be explained solely in terms of efficiency or by the interests of the most powerful states; they are in large part shaped by the opportunities and constraints created by institutional arrangements' (p.126).

The grounds for the need for institutional reform are clear. The pre-Nice institutional framework could be expected to lead to increased costs in the achievement of the EU objectives, mainly in the presence of enlargement, due to issue linkage created by the institutions[4]. For instance, if unanimity voting were maintained, the small, Southern member states could be placed in a position to trade their veto right for enhanced advantages or concessions, increasing thus the pressure - and costs - imposed on the larger existing member states.

Our analysis of the relationship between national and European objectives was equally revealing. The achievement of the single currency and price stability objectives seems to depend to a large extent on securing employment at national level. It seems that the (un)employment problem should have received more attention prior to the move to the single currency, besides the elements included in the Maastricht criteria[5]. This remains relevant for both the member states not in Euroland (the 'outs') and for any potential new member contemplating monetary integration.

The attainment of the price stability objective relates to the explicit role of the ECB in providing it, given that legal independence is an important determinant of inflation in the industrial countries (Cukierman, Webb and Neyapti 1992). In this respect EMU could be described as 'an efficient anti-inflationary commitment technology' (Eichengreen and Frieden, 1993)[6]. If the member states have the benefit of the ECB credibility, they can more successfully promote domestic polices focused on the unemployment problem.

At national level, however, a high level of employment secured through increased government expenditure appears to have a negative impact on growth (i.e. demand side policies)[7]. This may be linked to the shift, at European level, from a more activist policy towards a strategy based on medium term stability, market oriented policies and focus on measures devoted to enforcing the supply side of the economy, following the failure of macroeconomic policy coordination at the end of the 1970s and the decreasing confidence in the possibility of fine-tuning policy (Maes, 1996).

Our results indicate that national politics play a minor role in relationship to the achievement of objectives set outside national borders. It is not evident what this implies for the role played by interest groups in shaping the EMU outcome. Further analysis in this direction is important since, while not benefiting a particular country as a whole, EMU may nevertheless bring an improvement in the welfare of certain groups within the country, which prevail on the government to pursue their preferred policies. Based on anecdotal information, for instance, Eichengreen and Frieden (1993) argue that 'domestic distributional considerations are undoubtedly important, but have not yet been formulated in ways that allow us to arrive at clear conclusions as to their effects' (p.97).

The interaction between economic and political factors is equally relevant to policy-making in the EU. A high degree of government intervention at national level appears to have a negative impact on, *inter alia*, European trade and on fiscal policy which, as we have seen, are positively related to the introduction of the single currency. This implies a negative relationship between national government intervention and single currency. One can identify here support for the idea that those member states highly opposed to the loss of national sovereignty and, implicitly to the single currency (regarded as a symbol of European rather than national identity), are more in favour of 'diluting' the power centralisation at union level, through enlargement. This could explain, thus, the negative correlation between enlargement and fiscal policy and the implicit positive correlation between high levels of government intervention at national level and support for enlargement (rather than for the single currency).

At European level, price stability and employment emerge as more accessible objectives when political power centralisation is combined with a favourable impact of credibility on expectations. Price stability, credibility and expectations appear together in the literature devoted to central bank independence[8].

Grilli, Masciandro and Tabellini (1991) find that lower and less variable inflation is associated with central bank independence. Meanwhile, monetary regimes do not seem to matter for real economic performance (growth, unemployment) of for budgetary choices. Therefore, since political and monetary institutions determine fiscal and monetary discipline, which seem to be unrelated to each other, the credibility of EMU would be enhanced by fiscal rules that guaranteed the long-run solvency of the high debt countries. This is consistent with the introduction of the Stability and Growth Pact as a way of ensuring continuing budgetary discipline in the final stage of EMU.

Goodhart (1991) points out that, while it is generally true that more independent central banks have presided over less inflationary countries, it is also true that the public in these countries had a higher preference for price stability; that means that 'it is at least arguable that both the independence of the Central Bank and price stability have actually resulted from the more fundamental democratic concerns of the public, rather than that the independence has, by itself, guaranteed such price stability' (p.4).

We find that the objective of the single currency is positively related to high levels of trade and high standards of living. This could mean that the more open and developed member states are more likely to gain from the introduction of the single currency. Meanwhile, when regarded as a political objective (and thus considering the attached loss of national sovereignty), the single currency appears to have had, *ex ante*, a negative impact on both price stability and employment, which could very well reflect its impact on credibility and, through expectations on the real economy.

6.2. Single Currency

Most of the arguments related to the single currency have been explored on the basis of information available prior to 1 January 1999. They maintain, however, their relevance towards understanding the differences in *ex post* performance of the Euroland countries - the 'ins' - and towards evaluating the strategies of the 'outs'. Moreover, hopeful new member states that aim for monetary unification are to be assessed by the same set of criteria.

We find that the move to the single currency is more costly to those countries that are more exposed to asymmetric shocks and less able to adjust to such shocks. To be more specific, our results indicate that the cost of joining the single currency is likely to be higher for a country with a high inflation, low wage flexibility, which relies heavily on seigniorage revenue, borrows extensively from abroad and in which people regard money as a symbol of national identity.

The implication is that, by reducing inflation, eliminating seigniorage as a source of government income, decreasing foreign debt and promoting a more favourable image of the EU, countries are likely to diminish the expected costs of the move to the single currency. Save the last argument, the first elements are actually implicit or explicit in the Maastricht convergence criteria.

In other words, complying with the convergence criteria may be a way of reducing the costs of EMU rather than exacerbating them, in the spirit of the interpretation given by Winkler (1995) to the Maastricht criteria: reputation value for convergence (i.e. EMU's reputation is needed to induce convergence), convergence incentive for reputation (i.e. low-credibility countries require the promise and the benefit of EMU commitment, while the high-credibility countries require prior evidence of convergence to insure EMU reputation) and informational value of the behaviour they induce (i.e. through preference revealing and convergence of preferences).

As far as the adjustment to asymmetric shocks is concerned, increased labour mobility and enhanced wage flexibility are linked to a further reduction in the costs attached to the introduction of the single currency. According to Razin and Yuen (1996), one way of increasing labour mobility would be by lifting the implicit barriers, namely by privatising pension schemes and moving towards a portable social security and unemployment benefits scheme. Gros (1996) suggests a more flexible housing market as a reform of the labour market in preparing for EMU. As far as labour mobility is concerned, however, he points out that, besides its role as a short-run adjustment mechanism, it favours concentration of industry and hence increased potential for asymmetric shocks and pronounced core-periphery patters, with clear implications for multi-speed Europe.

The net favourable outcome can be increased both by reducing the costs and increasing the benefits. From our findings, ways of enhancing the benefits relate to improved growth performance, increased levels of trade with the other member states and reduced holdings of international reserves. Increased price stability (via credibility) and measures meant to discourage price discrimination (through European competition policy, e.g.) can also be added to the list.

The outcome of our quantitative analysis also points towards a multi-tier structure of the 'single currency EU15', with potential relative losers (Greece, Portugal, Spain, Italy) and potential relative gainers (Sweden, Finland, Ireland, Denmark, Luxembourg, UK, Austria, France, Belgium, Netherlands and Germany).

While some of the possible ways of improving the net outcome could be dealt with at national level (e.g. education, unemployment etc.), some others (e.g. labour mobility, competition policy, fiscal transfers) call for coordination and thus an European approach seems more suitable. The appropriate degree of centralisation of the instruments of economic policy (including both elements of coordination and harmonisation) depends on the spillover effects they provoke (Maes, 1996). The appropriateness of Community action is, by law, to be judged according to the subsidiarity principle[9], enshrined in the Maastricht Treaty (art. 3b), that functions should be allocated to the lowest level of government, unless welfare gains can be reaped by assigning it to the next higher level.

In this respect the distinctive characteristics (relative to the European average) of the potential gainers are relevant: higher growth, relatively lower attachment to the national currencies, higher levels of trade, lower inflation rates and more diversified industrial structures. In other words, a policy designed to promote trade, low inflation, industrial diversification and growth is likely to involve a net benefit from the move to the single currency.

Actual membership of the eurozone seems to have closest correlation to the attitude toward money as symbol of national identity, as well as to capital mobility, price discrimination and inflation rates. None of these elements have been prominent in the OCA literature in the way that labour mobility and wage flexibility have.

These findings are consistent with the literature supporting convergence as a prerequisite of the move to the single currency[10], on the grounds that a more homogenous Europe is less likely to lose from the move to the single currency. If poor economies or regions tend to grow faster than rich ones in per capita terms, in a neoclassical economy world, one would expect the EU member states to converge (Barro and Sala-i-Martin, 1992). How long this could take (before and after the move to the single currency) and to what extent such an outcome is undermined by differences in the steady-state characteristics requires further investigation[11].

A less favourable picture would develop in a world where path-dependency and location matter. In such a setting relative factor prices remain important, but additional factors can contribute to a different outcome. Within the framework set by the recent growth literature, the concentration of production in the more developed areas can be self-sustaining in the long run because such a concentration of production can be a sufficient condition for a process of cumulative growth differences between the core and the periphery.

When imperfect competition and increasing returns to scale are acknowledged, the issue of location becomes relevant: an increase in the productivity gap between the core and the periphery, an increase in the size of the manufacturing sector, stronger economies of scale, an increase in transportation costs - all would strengthen the initial centre-periphery pattern (Krugman, 1991). Meanwhile, the situation could be expected to reverse only in the presence of a substantial increase in transportation costs (to make location in the periphery desirable on profit maximisation grounds) and especially a reversal of the productivity gap (Brakman and Garretsen, 1993; Knell, 1995). Such arguments are relevant to both the single currency and the enlargement objectives.

6.3. ENLARGEMENT

The lack of homogeneity of the EU member states[12] in terms of economic, social and political characteristics could provide a good explanation of the often divergent interests displayed[13]. Divergent interests, in turn, make difficult the decision making process at European level and, thus, hinder the progress of the European integration process and hence the achievement of the objectives of the EU. Following this line of argument, convergence becomes a prerequisite for deeper integration.

According to our results, there seems to be a clear separation between the original core countries, the Scandinavian members and the Southern ones. This grouping, we find, is mainly related to the expectations about the national economy and its sustainable growth on the background of a strong sense of national integration. Our findings appear to indicate that the disparities among the current member states can be diminished mainly through the shaping of expectations about the EU as a whole and through government intervention directed towards achieving similar standards of living.

Further insight is gained when the potential EU members are taken into account. Overall, the clustering of the EU15 member states is maintained, while the CEECs tend to belong to a distinct group. On this basis one can hypothesise that the envisaged Eastern expansion is likely to enhance considerably the lack of internal homogeneity of the EU, with all the implications for a multi tier regional group.

6.4. MULTI-SPEED EUROPE

We found some evidence pointing at the possibility of a multi-speed evolution of the European integration process, given a *de facto* multi-tier structure of EU15. This characteristic is likely to be aggravated by the Eastern enlargement which, as our findings suggest and as Baldwin, Francois and Portes (1997) stress, 'will greatly increase the EU's economic diversity and thereby multiply the centrifugal forces' (p.150).

On the basis of economic, political and social characteristics we identify three distinct clusters of countries: the core (France, Italy, Germany and UK), the middle tier (the Benelux, the Scandinavian members, Austria and Ireland) and the periphery (Portugal, Spain and Greece)[14]. The main characteristics distinguishing between the three clusters relate to expectations about the national economy, growth and sense of national integration. The levels of intra-EU trade, employment, expectations about Europe, government intervention and standard of living are also of some importance.

Prima facie, national and European policies designed to reduce the disparities among the member states in terms of the identified discriminating characteristics would ensure increased homogeneity across the EU member states and therefore reduce the danger of a 'split' Europe.

Some authors regard a multi-speed Europe as an 'inevitability' (Eichengreen and Ghironi, 1995; Goodhart, 1996) with undesirable consequences for the process of European integration. Some argue that each member state should be given the right to decide whether to join or not, irrespective of the overall cost/benefit evaluation (e.g. De Grauwe, 1994a). Agnew (2001) goes as far as saying that changes in EU's approach to enlargement since the collapse of the communist bloc augurs a move 'away from a single Europe to a multi-tier, patchwork Europe with various "degrees" of actual membership' (p.30).

One drawback of such a variable geometry Europe relates to its potential for finding an equilibrium that permanently excludes the non-core member states, given the interest of the insiders to keep the number of EMU members small (Alesina and Grilli, 1993) and the desire of the outsiders to free-ride on the optimally chosen policy of the insiders (P. Martin, 1995). When the outsiders are small countries, their preferred outcome might be not to participate unless they can secure influence more than in proportion to their size (Casella, 1992) which, in turn, may not be acceptable for the larger, dominant partners. Another problem has to do with undermining the credibility of the whole process, especially if the idea of flexible architecture replaces the idea of *acquis communautaire* which, according to Martin (1993), 'has served as a signal of the members' intentions and linked their reputation to the EC in a way that informal or ad hoc agreements could not' (p.130).

Then, there is the danger of a disintegrating tendency, since the member states could chose to move forward independently, in a small group sharing common interests on narrowly defined topics, rather than aiming at mutually advantageous bargains across issues (Martin, 1993). Less credible links among issues would mean, in turn, reducing the costs of reneging and thus threatening the achievement of the EU objectives.

Along similar lines evolves also the argument of Viñals (1996) who regards an EMU going beyond the so-called core as a desirable option, since a wider EMU would not just seem appropriate on purely economic grounds but also necessary on political grounds, in order to preserve the integrity of the Single Market.

De Grauwe (1995a; 1996) finds that one of the main stumbling blocs for the low inflation countries (traditionally regarded as the core) to allow those member states following unorthodox fiscal policies in the union relate to the fear of the inflationary bias the latter could induce. He argues that by allowing the highly indebted countries into the union would make debt reduction targets easier to achieve and thus break the inflation-debt vicious circle. The conclusion would be, in De Grauwe's (1996) view, that a shift of focus away from convergence requirements and towards institutional strengthening of Europe's monetary institutions can be expected to increase the likelihood of Euroland becoming a zone of monetary stability, and provides a way of reducing the risk of a great and permanent division of the European Union.

Problems arise also in relation to the exchange rate between the euro and the currencies of the EU member states not included in EMU at the beginning of the third stage, with significant institutional implications (Spaventa, 1996; Eichengreen and Frieden, 1993).

One favourable view of the likely outcome of a two-speed Europe can be found in the argument of Von Hagen and Fratianni (1993): those EU core central banks, they say, that have an established reputation as committed to price stability in the past are expected to be reluctant to join in an EMU with less reputable central banks. As a consequence, the preferred solution for the core would be one that would allow them 'to retain a maximum degree of autonomy and the option to dissolve the EMU at a relatively low cost - i.e. an arrangement with decentralised objectives and operations, multiple currencies and a low degree of market integration' (p.181). As opposed to this scenario, the adopted two-speed approach, by allowing the core countries to proceed with EMU, in the end, would benefit the outsiders: while the non-core countries are 'concentrating' on increasing their convergence to the core, the core group 'would gain experience in the implementation of a unified EMU monetary policy. To the extent that this experience could be brought to bear when the peripheral countries joined the EMU, the two-speed approach would reduce information costs to these countries' (ibid, p.183). In retrospect, this argument maintains its relevance in relation to the progress of monetary integration in the eurozone and the CEECs awaiting accession. As far as the ins and the outs of EU15 are concerned, it seems that preferences regarding autonomy have prevailed over the signals from the application of strict economic convergence criteria.

Von Hagen and Fratianni (1993) warn that, as long as political integration is lacking, the EMU runs the risk of settling for 'merely a set of tightly coordinated, yet essentially national monetary strategies' (p.184) threatened by public dismay.

The stability of the whole structure is even more doubtful if one agrees with Goodhart's (1996) remark that, considering the experience of the disintegrating USSR, Yugoslavia or Czechoslovakia, the costs of withdrawing from a single currency and re-establishing separate currencies are not prohibitive. This is not true, though, according to Eichengreen and Frieden (1993) who believe that the cost of defecting from EMU, once in, will operate as an 'effective exit barrier' (p.89).

The crucial role played by the political side of the process is once more confirmed by Cohen (1993), who investigates the role played by economic, political and organisational factors in explaining the success or failure of a monetary union. He concludes that, while playing an important role, the appropriate economic conditions (high factor mobility, symmetric shocks) and organisational structures (an independent central bank, legal provisions for currency issue) remain of secondary importance in ensuring the longevity of a monetary union, since, historically, they have not always proved sufficient for holding a monetary union together. Instead, political factors appear to play a key role in preserving a MU over time: the presence of a dominant power (a hegemon) or sufficient political cohesion (a community) are crucial in neutralising the risk of time inconsistency on the side of sovereign governments faced with 'bargains that turn out to be inconvenient' (p.200).

It remains to be seen to what extent the political will for introducing the single currency and enlarging the EU towards the East will transform the European integration process from an ambitious project into an achievement.

NOTES

[1] Maes (1996) regards the tension between the logic of integration and the attachment to national sovereignty as one of the 'important continuities' at the European institutional level and lists a series of integration attempts that failed for this very reason.

[2] For the relevance of credibility, see the literature on speculative attacks (e.g. De Grauwe, 1994b).

[3] Recall that our results refer to relative net outcomes, whereas the views presented here refer to absolute results (in monetary terms).

[4] Eichengreen and Frieden (1993) define linkages as tying together of two otherwise unconnected issue areas, 'permitting the parties to an agreement to make concessions on one area in return for concessions on the other' (p.94); for example, the German agreement for monetary unification in exchange for the Community's acceptance of German unification in 1991. See also Garrett (1993) and Bofinger (1995).

[5] Jacques Chirac called, actually, in 1993, for tighter prerequisites for monetary union including the introduction of convergence in unemployment as a new criterion (Mélitz, 1995c).

[6] See also Alesina and Grilli (1992).

[7] For an exhaustive survey on the literature on European integration and growth see Baldwin and Seghezza (1996).

[8] While *political independence* refers to the capacity to chose the final goal of monetary policy (e.g. inflation, output), *economic independence* refers to the capacity to chose the instruments with which to pursue these goals. More specifically, the literature identifies economic independence with the autonomy to pursue the goal of low inflation (Grilli, Masciandro and Tabellini, 1991).

[9] This remains, as CEPR (1993) points out, a general principle rather than a source of explicit guidance. The concept and its application represent, according to Maes (1996), just another reflection of the tension between sovereignty and integration.

[10] See, among others, De Grauwe (1995b; 1996) for arguments in favour of the budgetary convergence requirements and against the nominal convergence criteria (inflation, interest rates, no devaluation). See also Douven and Engwerd (1993) and Prud'homme (1993).

[11] Barro and Sala-i-Martin (1992) investigate convergence within the framework of neoclassical growth models for closed economies; see Evans and Karras (1996) for an alternative approach. See also Button and Pentecost (1995) and, more recently, Dluhosch (2000).

[12] According to Knell (1995) these relate in principal to the diversity of institutional and industrial structures within Europe. See Prud'homme (1993) for a study of spatial disparities in EC12.

[13] Note that the argument 'in reverse' does not seem implausible, i.e. the lack of homogeneity could be due to divergent interests.

[14] By retaining the two clusters solution, a core-periphery pattern would emerge, with Greece, Spain and Portugal in the periphery and the remaining member states in an 'extended core'.

Chapter 7

Concluding Comments

7.1. Multivariate Statistics and Economic Analysis

Given that the analysis-of-variance group of techniques are most suitable in dealing with multidimensional phenomena, we found that the questions addressed provided a good opportunity of extending the use of such techniques to economics research. Among the objectives of scientific investigation for which multivariate methods are suited, we have been interested mainly in: data reduction or structural simplification (i.e. finding an optimum degree of simplicity, without sacrificing valuable information by *a priori* elimination of possibly relevant variables); sorting and grouping (i.e. using measured characteristics to identify groups including 'similar' objects); and investigation of the dependence among variables.

Until hypothesis testing along these lines becomes feasible in a dynamic framework, as far as hypothesis-making is concerned, our findings passed the test of validity suggested by Adelman and Morris (1970a), namely mutually consistent suggested hypotheses. On this basis we argue that multivariate statistical techniques are a valuable instrument, offering a method of investigation useful when traditional econometric analysis is not suitable, as it was the case with restricted (time series) data availability for the CEECs.

We regard our findings as an argument in favour of accepting these techniques as a valid choice for investigating economic phenomena, along with the more traditional ones. We strongly support the idea that methodological pluralism should not be dismissed on *a priori* grounds.

The repetition of our analysis after several years, when reliable time series data would have been built, should become a test for the robustness of both our findings and of the techniques employed.

7.2. THE FUTURE OF THE EUROPEAN UNION

As Varian (1996) puts it, '[P]art of the attraction and the promise of economics is that it claims to describe policies that will improve people's lives' (p.239). Throughout the research reported here we have been led by the desire to understand the transformations and challenges that Europe is facing, as a way towards identifying the choices which could help governments in finding the 'right' path.

The aim of this analysis was to investigate *empirically* the introduction of a single currency in the EU and the potential enlargement towards CEE, individually and in their interaction. We integrated the theoretical developments on regional economic and monetary integration developed before the Euro became reality and used them as the framework for our *exploratory* analysis.

We started by investigating the relationship between the EU objectives and instruments, the EU and the national objectives, and between the introduction of a single currency and the potential EU enlargement towards CEE. The analysis has been performed through CCA applied to factors extracted from a wide selection of economic, social and political characteristics of the EU 15 member states.

Our findings mainly suggest a possible trade-off between the two 'new' objectives (i.e. single currency and enlargement) and point out to the importance of dealing with unemployment in relationship to the introduction of the single currency - an aspect left out by the Maastricht convergence criteria.

Secondly, we investigated the spatial distribution of the potential gains and costs associated to the introduction of a single currency in the EU.

We employed FA as a way of concentrating a vast amount of information in few dimensions, as well as a way of extracting the latent factors contained in the data available (since most of the characteristics envisaged by the OCA literature are not directly measurable).

This allowed us to build a 'map' of the likely spatial distribution of the potential relative losers and gainers. We found that Germany emerges as a clear relative gainer, while Spain, Greece and Portugal can be easily identified as relative losers. The remaining eleven member states are clustered around the origin but, at a closer look, one can further distinguish Italy on the losers side, Benelux, France, UK, as well as Denmark and Austria, on the relative gainers side.

By estimating a discriminant function we could identify those country characteristics most likely to distinguish between potential losers and potential gainers. We found that not all the characteristics identified as relevant by the OCA literature are equally important in shaping the net outcome of the move to the single currency in Europe. More specifically, we found that high growth, regarding money as a symbol of national identity, elimination of transaction costs, openness and size of the economy, similarity of inflation rates, industrial diversification and goods markets integration emerge as decisive in separating potential gainers from potential losers.

Thirdly, on the basis of independent factors extracted from over one hundred economic, social, cultural and political variables we explored, through CA, the EU15 in terms of (dis)similarities across the member states. We found that at least three relatively homogenous groups of countries can be identified (the core, the Southern and respectively the Northern member states). When we then included in the analysis the potential candidates to EU membership (21 CEECs, Turkey and Cyprus), it appeared that the multi-tier structure of the EU is likely to be enhanced with an increase in the number of member states.

In the presence of a multi-tier structure of EU15 and with eleven of the fifteen member states proceeding to the introduction of the single currency, there is a possibility of a persistent 'elite' Euroland, centred on the core countries. This makes the possibility of all the existing member states having the same currency remote - unless the countries left out at the first stage agree to change their preferences, and pushes the prospect of a successful enlarged EU further into the future.

TECHNICAL APPENDIX

A1. FACTOR ANALYSIS

The following discussion in widely based on the introduction to Hotelling's principal component analysis (PCA) outlined by Krzanowski (1996). Given that factor analysis (FA) is PCA applied to standardised variables (Van de Geer, 1971), we shall depart from Krzanowski's terminology and refer to the principal components as factors.

Consider a data matrix (nxp) representing n points (countries in our case) in p dimensions (measured characteristics). If we consider the p-dimensional representation as the 'true' picture of the data, the purpose of FA is to obtain the 'best' r-dimensional representation ($r<p$) of the p-dimensional 'true' picture. In other words, FA offers a 'suitable projection method for viewing a high-multidimensional set of (quantitative) data in few dimensions' (Krzanowski, 1996, p. 63)[1].

Take a (px1) vector of variables $\mathbf{X}' = \left(X_1, X_2..X_p\right)$; let vector $\mathbf{x}_i$ denote the p values observed on the i-th case and let $\overline{\mathbf{x}}' = \left(\overline{x}_1, \overline{x}_2..\overline{x}_p\right)$ denote the sample mean vector. Let **S** be the sample covariance matrix, and $C=(n-1)S$ the corrected sum of squares and products matrix, where:

$$S = \frac{1}{n-1}\sum_{i=1}^{n}\left(x_i - \overline{x}\right)\left(x_i - \overline{x}\right)' \qquad (1)$$

Consider now a variable F defined as a linear combination of the original variables X. Its value corresponding to the i-th case will be:

$$f_i = a_1 x_{1i} + a_2 x_{2i} + \ldots + a_p x_{pi} = \mathbf{a'x}_i \tag{2}$$

Its mean will be $\overline{f} = \mathbf{a'\overline{x}}$, while its sample variance will be, using (1) and (2):

$$S^2{}_f = \frac{1}{n-1} \sum_{i=1}^{n} \left(f_i - \overline{f} \right) 2 = \mathbf{a'Sa} \tag{3}$$

where $\mathbf{a}' = \left(a_1, a_2, ..a_p \right)$ is a vector of coefficients of the *i*-th factor.

On this background we can define the *j*-th factor as the linear combination $F_j = \boldsymbol{a}'_j \boldsymbol{X}$ which has the greatest sample variance for all $\boldsymbol{a}_j$ satisfying:

$$\mathbf{a'}_j \mathbf{a}_j = 1 \quad \text{and} \quad \mathbf{a'}_j \mathbf{a}_i = 0, \quad i < j \tag{4}$$

(i.e., the eigenvectors are normalised to have unit sum of squared elements and are orthogonal to each other). Note that only the first constraint applies to the first factor.

Finding $\boldsymbol{a}_j$ amounts to finding F_j. Maximising the sample variance of F, namely (3), subject to (4) means maximising:

$$M_1 = \mathbf{a'}_1 \mathbf{Sa}_1 - l_1 \left(\mathbf{a'}_1 \mathbf{a}_1 - 1 \right) \tag{5}$$

that is to say solving:

$$\frac{\partial M_1}{\partial a_{1k}} = 0, \quad k = 1, 2, ..p$$

to obtain:

$$\mathbf{Sa}_1 = l_1 \mathbf{a}_1 \text{ or } \left(\mathbf{S} - l_1 \mathbf{I} \right) \mathbf{a}_1 = 0 \tag{6}$$

where l_1 (the Lagrange multiplier) is the eigenvalue of $\boldsymbol{S}$ and $\mathbf{a}_1$ its corresponding normalised eigenvector.

The value $a_{jk}/\sqrt{l_j}$ is called the *loading* of the *k*-th X on the *j*-th factor, while $f_{ij}=\mathbf{a'}_j\mathbf{x}_i$ is known as the i-th case *score* on the j-th factor. Also, from (6), $l_1 = \mathbf{a'}_1\,\mathbf{S}\mathbf{a}_1$. The first factor will have as coefficients the eigenvalues corresponding to the largest eigenvalue l_1.

The variance of the second component must be maximised after the first factor has been accounted for, and so on. Therefore, the *j*-th factor will be a linear combination of the *X*s which is orthogonal to all previous (*j*-1) components and which has maximum variance.

The proportion of the total variance explained by the first *r* factors gives a measure of the goodness of fit, P_r:

$$P_r = \frac{\sum_{i=1}^{n} l_i}{trace(\mathbf{S})} \tag{7}$$

There is no statistically justified lower limit of acceptability for P_r, but it is customary to regard factors that explain over 75% of the variation as an adequate representation of the true configuration.

A widely used indicator of sampling adequacy is the Kaiser-Meyer-Olkin (KMO) measure. This is computed as:

$$KMO = \frac{\sum\sum_{i \neq j} r_{ij}^2}{\sum\sum_{i \neq j} r_{ij}^2 + \sum\sum_{i \neq j} a_{ij}^2}, \tag{8}$$

where r_{ij} is the simple correlation coefficient between variables i and j; a_{ij} the partial correlation coefficient between variables i and j. The computed values indicate the degree of suitability of FA for the variables employed. More specifically, a small computed value means that FA may not be suitable, as correlations between pairs of variables cannot be explained by the other variables included (Norusis, 1994).

Testing for the number of factors that adequately represent the data in *k* dimensions can be achieved by testing H_0: $l_{k-1}=l_{k-2}=\ldots=l_p$, with a likelihood ratio test statistic[2] (Bartlett test):

$$W = n'(p-k)\ln\left(\frac{a}{g}\right) \sim \chi^2_{(p-k+2)(p-k-1)/2}\,, \tag{9}$$

where $n'=n-(2p+11)/6$ and:

$$a = \frac{\sum_{i=1}^{p} l_{k+i}}{p-k}; \quad g = \prod_{i=1}^{p}\left(l_{k+i}\right)^{\frac{1}{p-k}} \tag{10}$$

Customarily, factors with eigenvalues above one are retained. The interpretation of the factors is facilitated if one can distinguish the 'important' Xs from the 'unimportant' ones[3]. The distinction is based in practice on the size of the estimated coefficients, the unimportant Xs being those with estimated coefficients close to zero. Once more, there is no statistically justified way of deciding how small is 'small enough'. As far as the signs of the estimated parameters are concerned, the solution remains the same when they are reversed. The degree of subjectivity and arbitrariness in deciding upon the cutoff value brought much criticism to the technique which, otherwise, proves popular given the ease of the associated computations, the simple intuitive explanation and attractive properties of the factors extracted.

Given the problems with the formulation of appropriate hypotheses, the complicated or unavailable small sample theory and lack of clarity about when large sample theory becomes relevant, FA remains to be used most satisfactorily for descriptive purposes (Krzanowski, 1996). The composite measures extracted through FA can also be put to further use as variables in further statistical analysis[4] (see Sobel, 1994). In the latter case, in order to eliminate the problems brought by using data with different scales and magnitudes of measurement, the data is standardised and the sample covariance matrix $\boldsymbol{S}$ becomes the sample correlation matrix $\boldsymbol{R}$[5].

A2. Canonical Correlation Analysis

Take a set of variables (over n cases) divided, on external grounds, into two sets of p and q variables respectively. The aim of canonical correlation analysis (CCA) is to measure the association between the two collections of variables on the basis of the $(p+q)$x$(p+q)$ correlation matrix.

Consider one vector for each set of variables, $\boldsymbol{x}'=(x_1,x_2,...x_p)$ and $\boldsymbol{y}'=(y_1,y_2,...y_q)$. The objective is to find the largest possible correlation between two linear combinations $\mathbf{u}=\mathbf{a}'\mathbf{x}$ and $\mathbf{v}=\mathbf{b}'\mathbf{y}$. Note that for p=1 or q=1 CCA is equivalent to multiple regression analysis.

Given that:

$$corr(u,v)=\frac{\operatorname{cov}(u,v)}{\sqrt{[\operatorname{var}(u)][\operatorname{var}(v)]}}, \tag{11}$$

the maximum correlation is found by maximising $cov(u,v)$ subject to $var(u)=var(v)=1$. It can be shown (see Krzanowski, 1996) that the maximum (canonical) correlation is obtained as the square root of the largest eigenvalue of either the (pxp) matrix $\mathbf{E}_x=\mathbf{S}_{xx}{}^{-1}\mathbf{S}_{xy}\mathbf{S}_{yy}{}^{-1}\mathbf{S}_{yx}$ or the (qxq) matrix $\mathbf{E}_y=\mathbf{S}_{yy}{}^{-1}\mathbf{S}_{yx}\mathbf{S}_{xx}{}^{-1}\mathbf{S}_{xy}$, where

$$\mathbf{S}=\begin{bmatrix}\mathbf{S}_{xx} & \mathbf{S}_{xy}\\ \mathbf{S}_{yx} & \mathbf{S}_{yy}\end{bmatrix}$$

is the sample covariance matrix partitioned according to the two sets of variables.

Moreover, $\boldsymbol{a}$ is the eigenvector corresponding to the largest eigenvalue of $\boldsymbol{E}_x$, while $\boldsymbol{b}$ is the eigenvector corresponding to the largest eigenvalue of $\boldsymbol{E}_y$. There will be s pairs of canonical variates (variables) (u_i,v_i), $i=1,..s$ [where $s = rank(\boldsymbol{S}_{xy}) \leq min(p,q)$] that will quantify the association between $\boldsymbol{x}$ and $\boldsymbol{y}$ [$u_i=\boldsymbol{a}_i'\boldsymbol{x}$ and $v_i=\boldsymbol{b}_i'\boldsymbol{y}$, $i=1,..s$].

CCA transforms the p variables in $\boldsymbol{x}$ and the q variables in $\boldsymbol{y}$ to s pairs of canonical variables such that the u_is and v_is respectively are mutually uncorrelated and there is no cross-correlation besides $cov(u_i,v_i)=R_i$, $i=1,..s$.

The significance of the canonical correlation functions is often assessed using Pillai's criterion, among the most robust ones available. This is computed as

$$V=\sum_{i=1}^{s}\frac{1}{1+\lambda_i} \tag{12}$$

where λ_i is the i-th eigenvalue of the product between the hypothesis sum-of-squares and cross products matrix and the inverse of the error sum-of-squares and cross products matrix (Norušis, 1985).

The interpretation of the results is facilitated by standardising the variables prior to CCA; working with ***R*** will alter the canonical variates, but not the canonical correlations. Within these variates, the variables with large coefficients are the 'important' ones. The same criticism as before (see FA) applies with respect to subjectivity in choice of cutoff value.

One can also compute correlations between the canonical variates and the original variables; however, these only provide univariate information, while conveying nothing about how the original variables contribute jointly to the canonical analyses (Johnson and Wichern, 1992). The *k*-th squared canonical correlation (R_k^2) gives the proportion of the variance of the canonical variate *u* (or *v*) explained by *y* (respectively *x*) and is known as the shared variance between ***x*** and ***y***.

The results of CCA can be used for descriptive purposes, but are also suitable for inferential applications, under the assumption of multivariate normality. With ***x*** and ***y*** coming from a multivariate normal population with mean μ and correlation matrix ***P*** (with sample counterparts $\overline{x}$ and ***R***), one can make recourse to asymptotic results for the likelihood ratio statistic. It is, therefore, possible to test the null hypothesis of mutual independence of all variables [H_0: $\boldsymbol{P}=\boldsymbol{I}$; H_1: $\boldsymbol{P} \neq \boldsymbol{I}$] using

$$-n'\ln|R| \sim \chi^2_{\frac{1}{2}p(p-1)}; \quad n' = n - \frac{1}{6}(2p+11) \tag{13}$$

The determinant of ***R*** is equal to the product of its eigenvalues.

To test for no-association between ***x*** and ***y*** one can use

$$-2\ln\lambda = -n'\sum_{i=1}^{s}\ln\left(1-R^2_i\right) \sim \chi^2_{pq} \tag{14}$$

$n' = n-(p+q+3)/2$ (Krzanowski, 1996) or $n' = n-1-(p+q+1)/2$ (Johnson and Wichern, 1992).

The null hypothesis that the first *k* canonical correlations are non-zero can be tested using

$$-n'\sum_{i=k+1}^{s}\ln\left(1-R^2{}_i\right)\sim\chi^2{}_{(p-k)(q-k)} \qquad (15)$$

with $n' = n-(p+q+3)/2$.

A3. DISCRIMINANT ANALYSIS

Consider a matrix of standardised variables **X** (nxp) which is partitioned by rows into subgroups of observations. The aim of discriminant analysis (DA) is to specify (if existing) a compound score (discriminant function) of the variables that differentiates optimally between the subgroups.

Linear discriminant functions can be derived under the assumption of multivariate normality (essential for the reliability of findings) and equal population covariance matrices. The linear discriminant equation is similar to the multiple linear regression, with the vector of coefficients estimated so that the ratio of between-groups to within-groups sum of squares is maximised.

Let the matrix **X** (nxp) be partitioned in two submatrices X_1 (n_1xp) and X_2 (n_2xp), $n_1+n_2=n$, with the sample mean vectors $\overline{\mathbf{x}}_1$ and $\overline{\mathbf{x}}_2$. DA looks for the linear combination $d=\mathbf{a}'x$ that gives maximum separation of the group means when measured relative to the within group variance of the data. This can be found by maximising

$$\frac{\mathbf{a}'\left(\overline{\mathbf{x}}_1-\overline{\mathbf{x}}_2\right)^2}{\mathbf{a}'\mathbf{S}\mathbf{a}}$$

which leads to Fisher's linear discriminant function $d=\left(\overline{\mathbf{x}}_1-\overline{\mathbf{x}}_2\right)^2\mathbf{S}^{-1}\mathbf{x}$ (see Krzanowski, 1996).

Like in CCA, the first discriminant function provides the 'best' separation among groups; the second one, orthogonal to the first, separates best on the basis of associations not used in the first discriminant function. In general, for k groups there are (k-1) discriminant functions, uncorrelated to each other. The hypothesis of equal means on the discriminant function can be tested using Wilks' lambda. This gives the ratio of the within-group sum of squares (**W**) to the total sum of squares (i.e. the proportion of the total variance in the discriminant scores not explained by the differences among groups). Formally, it is given as:

$$\lambda = \prod_{i=1}^{p} (1+\theta_i)^{-1} \tag{16}$$

where θ_i are the eigenvalues of $\mathbf{W_0}^{-1}\mathbf{B_0}$, with:

$$\begin{aligned} \mathbf{W}_0 &= \sum_{i=1}^{g}\sum_{j=1}^{n_i}(\mathbf{x}_{ij}-\overline{\mathbf{x}}_i)(\mathbf{x}_{ij}-\overline{\mathbf{x}}_i)' \\ \mathbf{B}_0 &= \sum_{i=1}^{g} n_i(\overline{\mathbf{x}}_i-\overline{\mathbf{x}})(\overline{\mathbf{x}}_i-\overline{\mathbf{x}})' \end{aligned} \tag{17}$$

g is the number of random samples and $\overline{\mathbf{x}}$ is the mean for all n observations. (Krzanowski, 1996).

The coefficients estimated from standardised variables are interpreted similarly to the ones in FA or CCA: variables with large coefficients are thought to contribute more to the overall discriminant function[6]. However, the signs of the of the estimated coefficients are arbitrary.

One can also make use of the correlation between individual variables and the discriminant function (loadings). The same caveats apply as in the case of CCA[7].

A4. Cluster Analysis

Once more, consider a matrix of standardised variables **X** (nxp) with a corresponding symmetric and square (nxn) proximity matrix, whose cells include bilateral measures of (dis)similarity.

Cluster analysis (CA) represents a graphical method for examining such proximity matrices. It enables the construction of a configuration of n points where the distance between any two points is a measure of the dissimilarity between them, as well as a projection of such a configuration into a two-dimensional subspace. CA can be used to look for groups of relatively 'similar' units, which are relatively 'different' from all units in other groups.

The clustering process can be summarised diagrammatically in tree form (called *dendogram*). The diagram (see, e.g., Figure 5.1 in Chapter 5) shows the sequence of successive fusions or divisions that occur among existing groups as the value of dissimilarity at which two groups coalesce (clustering coefficient) varies between its extreme values. At one extremity all units form separate groups; at the other, all units belong to the same group. Graduation is indicated by an accompanying clustering coefficient scale.

One can 'cut' the dendogram (at a chosen number of groups or a chosen level of the clustering coefficient) to see which members (countries in our case) fall in which group.

There are numerous measures of (dis)similarity and various agglomerative algorithms[8]. We opted for the most popular one, Ward's method[9]. This produces a hierarchical CA which defines the dissimilarity between two clusters on the basis of the Euclidean distance. The measure used to reflect the tightness of any cluster C is given by the sum of squared Euclidean distances between the objects of the cluster and its centroids:

$$ESS(C) = \sum_{i \in C} \left\| x_i - \bar{x}(C) \right\|^2 . \tag{18}$$

The classification starts with each group (cluster) containing one observation. Successively, pairs of clusters are combined until the final point is reached, where all the observations (countries) join together, forming one large cluster. At each level of the hierarchy (moving towards right on the tree-diagrams) total ESS is considered. This represents the sum of all ESS(C) over all clusters at this level. The Ward method merges those clusters A and B between which the dissimilarity d(A,B) is minimal, where:

$$d^2(A,B) = \frac{2|A||B|}{|A|+|B|} \left\| \bar{x}(A) - \bar{x}(B) \right\|^2 \tag{19}$$

The increment in total ESS is given by:

$$\begin{aligned} \Delta ESS &= ESS(R) - ESS(A) - ESS(B) = \\ &= \sum_{i \in R} \left\| x_i - \bar{x}(R) \right\|^2 - \sum_{i \in A} \left\| x_i - \bar{x}(A) \right\|^2 - \sum_{i \in B} \left\| x_i - \bar{x}(B) \right\|^2 \end{aligned} \tag{20}$$

which can be reduced to:

$$\Delta ESS = \frac{1}{2} d^2(A,B) . \tag{21}$$

NOTES

[1] See Van de Geer (1971) for an extensive *n*-dimensional geometric presentation.

[2] This procedure generally leads to selection of values of *k* much larger than those chosen on the basis of the heuristic methods usually employed (Krzanowski, 1996).

[3] We follow the common practice of reporting the results obtained with varimax rotation, which attempts to minimise the number of variables that have high loadings on a factor and, therefore, ease interpretation.

[4] The interest in reducing data dimensionality can be also motivated by restrictions related to degrees of freedom.

[5] Note that the factors derived from ***R*** are not equal to those derived from ***S*** and that knowledge of one set of factors does not allow a simple transformation to the other set (Krzanowski, 1996).

[6] For two-group DA the estimated coefficients are proportional to the ones obtained by regressing the binary grouping variable on the *X*s (Norušis, 1994).

[7] Discriminant function coefficients are sometimes called canonical discriminant function coefficients.

[8] Given the computational costs, the divisive (as opposed to agglomerative) approach is not popular (it implies evaluating $2^{n-1}-1$ possible partitions for n cases). See Krzanowski (1996) for overview and examples.

[9] The Monte Carlo evidence on the superiority of its performance is mixed; however, see Milligan (1981).

Data Appendix

Countries:

Austria (AU), Belgium (BE), Denmark (DK), Finland (FN), France (FR), Germany (G), Greece (GR), Ireland (IR), Italy (IT), Luxembourg (LX), Netherlands (NT), Portugal (P), Spain (SP), Sweden (SW), United Kingdom (UK); Albania (AL), Armenia (AR), Azerbaijan (AZ), Belarus (BR), Bulgaria (BG), Croatia (CR), Czech Republic (CZ), Estonia (ET), Georgia (GE), Hungary (HU), Latvia (LT), Lithuania (LI), Macedonia (MA), Moldova (MO), Poland (PL), Russia (R), Romania (RO), Slovakia (SK), Slovenia (SV), Ukraine (UR), Yugoslavia (Y); Cyprus (CY), Turkey (TR).

Data:[1]

V1 = urban population as percentage in total population; 1994 (%)
V2 = total employment; 1994* (thousands)
V3 = primary school enrolment, females; 1993 (%)
V4 = primary school enrolment, males; 1993 (%)
V5 = secondary school enrolment, females; 1993 (%)
V6 = secondary school enrolment, males; 1993 (%)
V7 = tertiary enrolment ratio; 1993 (%)
V8 = percentage of illiterates; 1992* (%)
V9 = current educational expenditure as percentage of GNP; 1992* (%)
V10 = daily newspapers per 1000 inhabitants; 1992 (number)
V11 = television receivers per 1000 inhabitants; 1992 (number)
V12 = radio receivers per 1000 inhabitants; 1992 (number)

V13 = percentage of the population speaking the national language (%)
V14 = percentage of population belonging to the predominant religion (%)
V15 = predominant religion: 1 = Roman Catholic; 2 = Evangelical Lutheran; 3 = Protestant; 4 = Orthodox; 5 = Muslim; 6 = Judaism; 7 = Shinto; 8 = Anglican.
V16 = total number offenders; 1990 ('000)
V17 = crude fertility rate; 1994 (number)
V18 = percentage of pupils in general secondary education learning English as a foreign language; 1991-92 (%)
V19 = percentage of pupils in general secondary education learning French as a foreign language; 1991-92 (%)
V20 = percentage of pupils in general secondary education learning German as a foreign language; 1991-92 (%)
V21 = percentage of the population who can speak English except as mother tongue (%)
V22 = percentage of the population who can speak French except as mother tongue (%)
V23 = percentage of the population who can speak German except as mother tongue (%)
V24 = percentage of women in the labour force; 1994 (%)
V25 = infant mortality rate; 1994 (number per 1000 live births)
V26 = kilo-calories per caput per day; 1992 (number)
V27 = energy consumption per capita; 1992 (thousand metric tons of coal equivalent and kg/capita)
V28 = hospital beds per 1000 population; 1985-90 (number)
V29 = expenditure on social security and welfare as percentage of total central government expenditure; 1994* (%)
V30 = number of human rights conventions to which the country is a party (out of a total of 23); 1994 (number)
V31 = percentage of population in favour of the single currency; 1995 (%)
V32 = social services as percentage of total government expenditure; 1994 (%)
V33 = transfers from the central government to other levels of national government as percentage of central government expenditure; 1994* (%)
V34 = dummy variable on the type of organisation of government: 1 = nascent/evolving democracy; 2 = republic; 3 = constitutional/parliamentary monarchy; 4 = federal republic; 5 = president parliamentary government; 6 = confederation with parliamentary democracy; 7 = (republican) parliamentary democracy.
V35 = number of parties in government; 1955-89 (annual mean; number)

V36 = government ideology index; five point scale coded as it follows: 1 = for governments in which a right-wing party or set of parties controls all ministries in a particular year; 2 = if right-wing parties control between 2/3 and 99% of all ministries; 3 = if neither right-wing nor left-wing government control more than 2/3 of all ministries; 4 = left-wing control of between 66 and 99%; 5 = left wing dominance.
V37 = Royed/Borrelli strength of government index
V38 = assembly size: total number of seats in the legislature
V39 = effective threshold for representation
V40 = effective number of elective parties
V41 = effective number of parliamentary parties
V42 = total number of members in cabinet
V43 = total number of parties in cabinet
V44 = type of cabinet dummy variable: 1 = single party majority; 2 = single party minority; 3 = minimum winning coalition; 4 = minority coalition; 5 = oversized coalition
V45 = mean scores for cabinet portfolios as policy payoffs or office payoffs;
V46 = ideology dummy: -2 = left wing government; -1 = centre-left; 0 = centre; 1 = centre-right; 2 = right wing government
V47 = defence expenditure as percentage of total expenditure; 1994* (%)
V48 = military expenditure as percentage of GNP; 1989* (%)
V49 = R&D expenditure as % of GDP; 1994 (%)
V50 = R&D personnel as percentage of labour force; 1994 (%)
V51 = percentage of gross domestic expenditure on R&D performed by the government sector: 1995* (%)
V52 = inventivity coefficient: resident patent applications per 1000 population; 1993
V53 = general government consumption as percentage of GDP; 1994 (%)
V54 = participation in European decisions: percentage of population considering that European citizens do have a say in the decisions of the European Union; 1996
V55 = satisfaction with democracy in European Union: percentage of people who answered 'very satisfied' and 'fairly satisfied' when asked : 'On the whole, are you very satisfied, fairly satisfied, not very satisfied or not at all satisfied with the way democracy works in the European Union?'; 1996
V56 = satisfaction with democracy in own country: percentage of people who answered 'very satisfied' and 'fairly satisfied' when asked : 'On the whole, are you very satisfied, fairly satisfied, not very satisfied or not at all satisfied with the way democracy works in (our country)?'; 1996

V57 = European Parliament Elections turnout, 1994, (%)
V58 = percentage of people regarding themselves as 'Europeans' in the near future; 1996 (%)
V59 = percentage of people regarding themselves as 'nationals' only; 1996 (%)
V60 = percentage of population feeling attached to one's country; 1996 (%)
V61 = percentage of population in favour of a Federal European Union; 1996 (%)
V62 = percentage of population expecting an enlargement of the European Union to take place by the year 2010; 1996 (%)
V63 = percentage of EC directives implemented by nation states; 1996 (%)
V64 = percentage of population in favour of 'one country, one vote' in the EU Council of Ministers; (%)
V65 = qualified majority in the Council of the EU (number of votes)
V66 = number of seats in the European parliament (number)
V67 = origin of the 222 members of the Committee of the Regions (number)
V68 = number of Commissioners (number)
V69 = subsidiarity: percentage of people who agree that 'The European Union should be responsible for matters that cannot be effectively handled by national, regional and local governments' ;1996 (%)
V70 = feeling informed: percentage of population answering 'very well' and 'quite well' when asked: 'All things considered, how well informed do you feel you are about the European Union, its policies and its institutions?'; 1996 (%)
V71 = percentage of population regarding EU membership as a 'good thing'; 1996 (%)
V72 = hours of news on the main national TV (per year); 1992
V73 = news as percentage of TV programme output on the main national TV; 1993* (%)
V74 = share of agriculture in GDP 1994 (%)
V75 = GNP per capita (dollars) 1994
V76 = average annual growth of GNP per capita; 1985-94 (%)
V77 = share of gross domestic investment in GDP; 1994 (%)
V78 = average annual growth rate of gross domestic investment; 1990-94 (%)
V79 = share of industry in GDP; 1994 (%)
V80 = harvester-threshers in use; 1993 (number)
V81 = milking machines in use; 1993 (number)
V82 = tax revenues as percentage of GNP; 1994 (%)
V83 = non-tax revenue as percentage of GNP; 1994 (%)
V84 = total revenue as percentage of GNP; 1994 (%, V89 + V90)
V85 = gross domestic savings as percentage of GDP; 1994 (%)

V86 = loans granted by the EIB; between 1990-94 (mil ECU)
V87 = loans granted by the EIB as percentage of total loans within EU
V88 = share of manufacturing in total exports; 1993 (%)
V89 = percentage of intra-industry trade with the EC; 1988-90 (%)
V90 = population; mid-1994 (million)
V91 = total surface area, comprising land area and inland waters ('000 sq. km)
V92 = total labour force; 1994 (millions)
V93 = imports from EC12; 1993 (mill ECU)
V94 = exports to EC12; 1993 (mill ECU)
V95 = average annual rate of inflation measured by the rate of change in the GDP implicit deflator; 1984-94 (%)
V96 = carbon dioxide emissions per capita; 1992 (metric tones)
V97 = average annual deforestation of natural forest area; 1981-90 (%)
V98 = naturally protected areas as percentage of total surface area; 1994 (%)
V99 = consumer price index, 1993; 1980=100 (%)
V100 = railway network at end of year; 1991/93 (km)
V101 = road network at end of year; 1992/93 (km)
V102 = roads density (km/1000 sq. km)
V103 = airports (number)
V104 = cereals production, total; 1994 (1000 mt)
V105 = total production of vegetables; 1994 (1000 mt)
V106 = total fruit production; 1994 (1000 mt)
V107 = total meat production from slaughtered animals; 1994 (1000 mt)
V108 = aggregate legal central bank independence; 1980-89
V109 = gross international reserves; 1994 (mill $)
V110 = financing of the 1995 general budget by member state, payment appropriations; 1995 (%)
V111 = appropriations for the structural funds by member state; 1994-99 (mil ECU at 1994 prices)
V112 = financing from monetary authorities as a percentage of total expenditure and lending minus repayments; 1994* (%)
V113 = inflow of asylum seekers; 1994* (thousands)
V114 = stock of foreign labour; 1993* (thousands)
V115 = unemployment total, 1994, (mil)
V116 = correlation of supply disturbances with changes in terms of trade
V117 = size of supply disturbances
V118 = adjustment speed to supply disturbances
V119 = size of demand disturbances
V120 = adjustment speed to demand disturbances

V121 = yield on fixed interest securities, central government, yearly average, 1994
V122 = central bank advance rates on securities, December 1994
V123 = central government foreign debt, end 1993, mil ECU
V124[2] = short-run divergence in inflation rate
V125[3] = long-run divergence of inflation rates
V126[4] = share of trade in GDP
V127[5]= share of exports to EC12 in total exports
V128[6] = share of imports from EC-12 in total imports
V129 = magnitude of intra-industry trade (Grubel coefficient)
V130 = average propensity to import
V131 = marginal propensity to import
V132 = official gross reserves of convertible currencies, mil ECU
V133[7] = real wage flexibility
V134 = uncertainty avoidance index
V135 = seigniorage revenue as share of GDP (%)

SOURCES

Baldwin, R. E. (1992). The economic logic of EFTA countries joining the EEA and the EC, *EFTA Occasional Paper*, no.41 (V129);

Banks, A. S. (ed.) (1995). *Political Handbook of the World, 1994*; CSA Publications, New York (V38, V39, V42, V43, V44, V46);

Bayoumi, T. and B. Eichengreen (1994). *One money or many? Analyzing the prospects for Monetary Unification in various parts of the world*, Princeton Studies in International Finance, no.76 (V116, V117, V118, V119, V120);

Borrelli, S. A and T. J. Royed (1995). Government 'strength' and budget deficits in advanced democracies, *European Journal of Political Research*, vol.28, no.2, pp.225-260 (V35, V36, V37);

Buigues P. and F. Ilzkowitz (1992). *Central and Eastern European Communities Basic Facts and Main Issues: Trade*, Commission of the EC, DGII, doc11/125/95en (V89);

CEPR (1995), *Flexible integration: towards a more effective and democratic Europe*, Monitoring European Integration (V57, V68);

Cukierman, A. et al. (1992). Measuring the independence of central banks and its effects on policy outcomes; *The World Bank Economic Review*, vol.6, no.3, pp.353-398 (V108);

Hofstede, G. (1990). Motivation, leadership and organization: do American theories apply abroad?, in D.S. Pugh (ed.), *Organization theory: selected readings*, Penguin Books (V134);

Koole, R. and P. Mair (1993). Political data in 1992, *European Journal of Political Research*, vol.24, no.4, Political data Yearbook 1993 (V43, V44, V45);

Laver, M. and B. W. Hunt (1992). *Policy and Party Competition*, New York and London, Routledge (V45);

Lijphart, A. (1994). *Electoral Systems and Party Systems: a Study of Twenty-Seven Democracies 1954-1990*, Oxford University Press (V38, V39, V40, V41);

Neven, D. (1994). The political economy of state aids in the European Community: some econometric evidence, *CEPR Discussion Paper*, no. 945 (V46);

Reddy, M. A (ed.) (1994). *Statistical Abstract of the World*, Gala Research Inc. (V8, V10, V11, V12, V16, V28, V34, V48, V91, V92, V103);

Spahn, B. (1993). The consequences of economic and monetary union for fiscal federal relations in the Community and the financing of the Community budget, *European Economy*, no.5, (V135);

*** *Annual Bulletin of Transport Statistics for Europe and North America*, 1995 (V100, V101, V102);

*** *Central and Eastern Eurobarometer*, no.6, March 1996 (V13, V14, V15);

*** Council of Europe (1994/95), *Cinema, Television, Video and New Media in Europe Statistical Yearbook* (V72, V73);

*** *Eurobarometer*, 44, Spring 1996 (V60, V61, V62);

*** *Euromonitor*, 44, Spring 1996 (V13, V14, V15, V21, V22, V23, V64, V65, V66, V67, V69);

*** *European, The,* 25-31 July 1996 (V63);

*** *Europinion*, no.8, March 1996 (V54, V55, V56, V58, V59, V70, V71);

*** Eurostat (1995). *Basic Statistics of the European Union*, 32nd ed. (V93, V94);

*** Eurostat (1995). *Europe in Figures*, 4th ed. (V18, V19, V20, V49, V50, V86, V87, V93, V94, V110, V111);

*** FAO (1994). *Yearbook*, vol.48 (V7, V80, V81, V104, V105, V106, V107);

*** *Flash Eurobarometer*, 16-20 December 1995 (V31);

*** IMF (1994, 1995). *Government Finance Statistics Yearbook* (V29, V30, V33, V112);

*** International Labour Office (1995). *Yearbook of Labour Statistics* (V2);

*** OECD (1995). *Trends in International Migration Annual Report*, 1994 (V113, V114);

*** OECD (1996). *Main Science and Technology Indicators* (V51, V52);

*** United Nations (1993). *Statistical Yearbook*, 40th issue (V9, V10, V11, V12, V27, V115);

*** World Bank (1996). *World Development Report* (V1, V3, V4, V5, V6, V7, V17, V24, V25, V26, V28, V32, V47, V53, V74, V75, V76, V77, V78, V79, V82, V83, V84, V85, V88, V90, V95, V96, V97, V98, V109)

NOTES

[1] *indicates that for some countries the data refers to a year close to the one indicated

[2] This is calculated as the average of the yearly standard deviations of the national inflation rates from the German inflation rates (based on consumer price index; 1970-1994);

[3] This is calculated as the standard deviation of the average national inflation rates from the German inflation rates (based on consumer price index; 1970-1994);

[4] computed

[5] computed

[6] computed

[7] estimated as in Commission of the EC (1990)

FACTORS APPENDIX

Factor	Name	Description	Variable	Loadings for the first two factors	
F1; F2	investment in human capital (education expenditure); human capital potential (enrolment ratio);	relates high levels of education and R&D expenditure to high levels of primary school enrolment; reflects the available human capital 'under preparation';	V3	**-0.88976**	-0.11432
			V4	**-0.87731**	-0.11314
			V49	**0.69024**	-0.04890
			V9	**0.56471**	0.09763
			V7	**0.56429**	**0.55988**
			V5	0.00911	**0.97106**
			V6	0.06970	**0.90690**
F3; F4	government intervention (European dimension); government intervention (domestic dimension)	illustrates government presence, considering access to European resources as well; illustrates the relationship between government revenue and expenditure, at domestic level;	V86	**0.86810**	-0.01611
			V109	**0.84227**	-0.00714
			V83	**-0.64769**	**0.63927**
			V53	-0.19867	**0.90402**
			V82	-0.15656	**-0.78911**
F5; F6	media penetration - national (expectations); media use - national (expectations);	illustrates the extent to which various media means are spread, making information accessible to the public; reflects the extent of using media as a means of influencing expectations (through news);	V12	**0.90910**	0.03443
			V11	**0.90410**	-0.13023
			V10	**0.75231**	-0.39930
			V73	-0.02868	**0.97175**
			V72	-0.22636	**0.93841**
F7; F8	media penetration - European (expectations);	same with F5; F6, at European level;	V11	**0.88076**	0.21015
			V12	**0.82852**	0.21401
			V10	**0.79265**	0.10710
			V71	**-0.68967**	**0.53875**
			V70	0.29230	**0.86403**

Factor	Name	Description	Variable	Loadings for the first two factors	
F9; F10	actual investment;	reflects the actual level and growth of	V77	**0.94743**	0.04687
	investment potential;	investment;	V78	**0.90701**	-0.18706
		reflects the potential for investment	V85	0.04223	**0.88733**
		(income and savings);	V75	-0.16850	**0.82710**
F11	EU trade;	indicates the intensity/strength of trade	V93	**0.95130**	
		relationships between the member	V94	**0.94783**	
		states;	V89	**0.83333**	
			V88	0.49287	
F12; F13	standard of living (urban	reflects various aspects of urban life	V96	**0.88184**	0.08127
	life);	(from access to information to levels of	V18	**0.70976**	-0.03011
	standard of living (health);	pollution);	V1	**0.70540**	0.23220
		relates high levels of health care to	V11	**0.69123**	**0.51276**
		healthy nutrition and low mortality;	V12	**0.67920**	**0.55484**
			V10	**0.61335**	**0.59404**
			V26	-0.12164	**-0.88675**
			V25	-0.12827	**-0.85389**
			V27	0.04966	**0.60483**
			V28	0.27182	**0.54253**
F14	(un)employment;	reflects the relationship between high	V95	**0.92130**	
		price stability and income growth and	V75	**-0.86411**	
		low levels of unemployment;	V99	**0.84558**	
			V115	-0.13035	
F15; F16	national identity;	reflects the degree of attachment to	V60	**0.93588**	0.03853
	national integration;	national values (beliefs, language,	V61	**-0.85048**	-0.24336
		religion);	V14	**0.61012**	**-0.63054**
		reflects the strength of the relationship	V13	**0.51892**	**0.51227**
		between central and local government;	V33	0.21119	**0.73056**
			V59	0.04653	**0.71832**

Factor	Name	Description	Variable	Loadings for the first two factors	
F17	democracy (national and European level);	reflects the extent of satisfaction with the degree of individual participation in decisions at both European and national level;	V55	**0.84564**	
			V54	**0.69608**	
			V30	**-0.65321**	
			V56	**0.51422**	
F18; F19	sustainable growth from technological change; sustainable growth from income;	reflects growth based on technological change and respecting the environment; reflects growth from high income consistent with environment protection;	V49	**0.95984**	0.07566
			V52	**0.91427**	**0.63044**
			V50	**0.88636**	0.24966
			V51	**-0.66725**	0.44664
			V98	**0.50590**	0.17402
			V97	-0.07058	**0.84329**
			V79	0.12999	**0.83619**
			V76	**-0.51769**	**-0.78324**
F20	military expenditure	reflects the trade-off between military expenditure and expenditure on welfare	V48	**0.91671**	
			V29	**-0.84015**	
			V47	**0.80996**	
			V32	**-0.77971**	
F21; F22	government stability; ideology;	reflects the degree of stability of the governing body and its policy; reflects the significance of ideological orientation and its relationship to political stability;	V40	**0.89996**	-0.25638
			V41	**0.88107**	-0.36108
			V37	**0.87034**	-0.06379
			V35	**0.84720**	-0.16507
			V44	**0.80296**	0.22274
			V43	**0.80088**	0.17082
			V39	**-0.53580**	0.42707
			V34	-0.47759	-0.31723
			V38	-0.11066	**0.76081**
			V46	0.03206	**0.72745**
			V42	0.04600	**0.66167**
			V45	-0.22200	**0.58811**

Factor	Name	Description	Variable	Loadings for the first two factors	
			V36	-0.25157	-0.29403
F23; F24	European identity;	reflects the degree of attachment to	V57	**0.89451**	-0.27161
	European integration;	European values;	V59	**-0.78499**	-0.32310
		reflects the degree of agreement and	V58	**0.76737**	0.28759
		commitment to European integration;	V54	-0.04527	**0.82611**
			V55	0.21169	**0.75800**
			V63	0.05151	**0.51765**
			V64	0.36765	**0.50226**
F25; F26	Eastern enlargement	reflects the dominant attitude towards	V59	**0.85953**	0.21424
	(expectations);	EU membership;	V70	**0.63665**	-0.08117
	Eastern enlargement	reflects the attitude towards	V36	**0.53827**	-0.16637
	(attitude);	enlargement in terms of dominant	V46	-0.03903	**-0.82025**
		interests;	V74	-0.04447	**0.70877**
			V54	**-0.53442**	**0.61634**
F27; F28	single market (cultural	reflects the degree of elimination of	V21	**0.90382**	0.18700
	integration);	language barriers;	V23	**0.86192**	-0.30758
	single market (freedom of	reflects the achieved degree of	V20	**0.76257**	-0.24882
	movement);	mobility within the EU;	V18	**0.62412**	**0.59080**
			V114	-0.25975	**0.82614**
			V19	-0.05795	**-0.65447**
			V113	0.04537	**0.57916**
			V22	0.22194	-0.49642
F29	political power	reflects the level of development of	V66	**0.99135**	
	centralisation (European	European institutions, as European vs.	V67	**0.98843**	
	institutions);	national representation;	V65	**0.98610**	
			V68	**0.97017**	
			V69	0.44013	
F30	fiscal policy;	illustrates the importance of the fiscal	V111	**0.88960**	

Factor	Name	Description	Variable	Loadings for the first two factors	
		policy, at national and European level;	V84	**-0.81763**	
			V110	**0.53538**	
F31	price stability;	reflects the degree of commitment to price stability (and the importance of independent monetary policy);	V112	**0.91848**	
			V99	**0.91071**	
			V95	**0.88336**	
			V108	0.24764	
F32	single currency;	reflects the importance attached (at national level) to the single currency;	V95	**0.92882**	
			V99	**0.80639**	
			V31	**-0.67013**	
			V93	-0.44039	
F33	factor endowment;	illustrates the growth potential (in terms of resources available, natural and infrastructure);	V100	**0.97258**	
			V92	**0.94262**	
			V90	**0.94324**	
			V101	**0.97285**	
			V107	**0.91276**	
			V104	**0.94282**	
			V103	**0.90192**	
			V91	**0.69325**	
			V102	0.43489	
F34; F35	nationally differentiated shocks (speed of adjustment to supply disturbances);	illustrates the trade-off between size of asymmetric shocks and speed of adjustment (supply and demand side);	V117	**-.89392**	.31996
			V115	**.82759**	.41183
			V119	.33152	.20312
			V116	-.07572	**.90263**
			V120	.41784	**.76308**
F36	similarity of inflation rates;	contains information reflecting both short run and long run divergence of inflation rates among member states;	V124	**.99651**	
			V125	**.99651**	
F37; F38	openness and size of the	reflects the importance of trade in	V130	**.98500**	.01951

Factor	Name	Description	Variable	Loadings for the first two factors	
	economy;	general and intra-EU in particular, for each member state;	V131	**.98366**	-.01844
			V126	**.90295**	.33340
			V129	.10216	**.84683**
			V128	.29893	**.74750**
			V127	.09300	**-.68776**
F39	capital mobility;	illustrates the relationship between interest rates and capital inflows;	V121	**.76605**	
			V122	**-.60992**	
			V123	**.59932**	
F40	money as symbol of national identity;	illustrates the importance attributed to money as a symbol of sovereignty;	F21	**.84149**	
			F23	**.84149**	
F41; F42	industrial diversification and goods market integration;	indicated the degree of diversification of the member states' industrial structure;	V88	**.86686**	.36887
			V135	**.78341**	**-.51792**
			V129	.06769	**.94530**
F43	wage flexibility;	illustrates the natural adjustment mechanism in the member states economies;	V133	**-.90360**	
			V95	**.76124**	
			V115	.39589	
F44; F45	labour mobility;	indicates the degree of labour mobility within the EU considering both economic incentives and cultural barriers;	V75	**.88941**	.17229
			V95	**-.87251**	-.03900
			V99	**-.76015**	-.16790
			F24	**.65395**	-.42212
			V114	.00299	**.90760**
			V113	.33625	**.76369**
			V115	-.09426	**.75721**
			F26	.07324	.07939
F46	loss of seigniorage revenue;	indicates the importance of seigniorage revenue in the member states;	V112	**.83107**	
			V135	**.83107**	
F47	risk elimination;	indicates the relationship between the level of investment and attitude	V77	**.93254**	.18499
			V134	**.85257**	-.39195

Factor	Name	Description	Variable	Loadings for the first two factors	
		towards risk;	V85	-.02833	**.98004**
F48	elimination of transaction costs;	indicated the importance of trade among the member states;	V93	**.95130**	
			V94	**.94783**	
			V89	**.83333**	
			V88	.49287	
F49	elimination of information costs and price discrimination;	reflects price divergence and price elasticity across the member states;	V135	**.92444**	
			V128	**.80980**	
			V127	**.51986**	
			V124		
F50	lower official international reserves.	indicates the current importance of official international reserves in the member states.	V132	**.95076**	
			V122	**.93923**	
			V126	-.18418	

REFERENCES

Abbott, A. (2001). Exchange rate variability and trade, in Lawler, K. and H. Seddighi (eds.), *International economics: theories, themes and debates*, Pearson Education.

Adelman, I., M. Geier and C. T. Morris (1969). Instruments and goals in economic development, *American Economic Review*, vol.59, no.2, pp.409-426.

Adelman, I. and C. T. Morris (1965). A factor analysis of the interrelationship between social and political variables and per capita gross national product, *Quarterly Journal of Economics*, vol.79, no.4, pp.555-578.

Adelman, I. and C. T. Morris (1970a). Factor analysis and gross national product: a reply, *Quarterly Journal of Economics*, vol.84, no.4, pp.651-662.

Adelman, I. and C. T. Morris (1970b). An econometric model of development: reply, *American Economic Review*, vol.60, part 1, pp.236-248.

Adelman, I. and C. T. Morris (1971a). Analysis-of-variance techniques for the study of economic development, *Journal of Development Studies*, vol.8, no.1, pp.91-105.

Adelman, I. and C. T. Morris (1971b). *Society, politics and economic development: a quantitative approach*, Baltimore, John Hopkins Press.

Adelman, I. and C. T. Morris (1973). *Economic growth and social equity in developing countries*, Stanford University Press.

Agnew, J. (2001). How many Europes? The European Union, eastward enlargement and uneven development, *European Urban and Regional Studies*, vol.8, pp.29-38.

Alesina, A. and V. Grilli (1992). The European Central Bank: reshaping monetary politics in Europe; in: M. B. Canzoneri, V. Grilli and P. R. Masson (eds.),

Establishing a central bank: issues in Europe and lessons from the US, Cambridge University Press.

Alesina, A. and V. Grilli (1993). On the feasibility of a one-speed or multi-speed European Monetary Union, *Economics and Politics*, vol.5, no.2, pp.145-165.

Alesina, A. and N. Roubini (1994). Political cycles in OECD economies, in T. Persson and G. Tabellini (eds.), *Monetary and Fiscal Policy*, vol.2: Politics, MIT Press.

Alesina, A. and L. H. Summers (1993). Central Bank Independence and macroeconomic performance, *Journal of Money, Credit and Banking*, vol.25, no.2, pp.151-162.

Alogoskoufis, G. and R. Portes (1992). European Monetary Union and international currencies in a tripolar model, in: M. B. Canzoneri, V. Grilli and P. R. Masson (eds.), *Establishing a central bank: issues in Europe and lessons from the US*, Cambridge University Press.

Anderton, R., R. Barrell and J. McHigh (1992). Nominal convergence in European wage behaviour: achievements and explanations, in R. Barrell (ed.), *Economic convergence and Monetary Union in Europe*, Sage Publications.

Arestis, P., A. Brown, K. Mouratidis and M. Sawyer (2002). The Euro: reflections on the first three years, *International Review of Applied Economics*, vol.16, no.1, pp.1-17.

Åslund, A. (1991). Systemic change in Eastern Europe and East-West trade, *EFTA Occasional Paper*, no.31.

Backus, D. and J. Driffill (1985). Rational expectations and policy credibility following a change in regime, *Review of Economic Studies*, vol.52, no.2, pp.193-203.

Baldwin, R. E. (1992). The economic logic of EFTA countries joining the EEA and the EC, *EFTA Occasional Paper*, no.41.

Baldwin, R. E. (1993a). The potential for trade between countries of EFTA and Central and Eastern Europe, *EFTA Occasional Paper*, no.44.

Baldwin, R. E. (1993b). A domino theory of regionalism, *CEPR Discussion Paper*, no.857.

Baldwin, R. E. (1995). The Eastern Enlargement of the EU, *European Economic Review*, vol.39, no.3-4, pp.474-481.

Baldwin, R. E; J. F. Francois and R. Portes (1997). The costs and benefits of eastern enlargement: the impact on the EU and central Europe, *Economic Policy*, no.4, pp.125-176.

Baldwin, R.E. and E. Seghezza (1996). Growth and European Integration: towards an empirical assessment, *CEPR Discussion Paper*, no.1393.

Banking Federation of the European Union (1995). *Survey on the introduction of the single currency: a first contribution on the practical aspects.*

Barro, R. J. and D. B. Gordon (1983). Rules, discretion and reputation in a model of monetary policy, *Journal of Monetary Economics*, vol.12, pp.101-121.

Barro, R. J. and X. Sala-i-Martin (1992). Convergence, *Journal of Political Economy*, vol.100, no.2, pp.223-251.

Barro, R. J. and X. Sala-i-Martin (1995). *Economic growth*, McGraw Hill.

Bayoumi, T. (1994). A formal model of optimum currency areas, *CEPR Discussion Paper*, no.968.

Bayoumi, T. and B. Eichengreen (1992). Is there a conflict between EC enlargement and European monetary unification?, *CEPR Discussion Paper*, no.646.

Bayoumi, T. and B. Eichengreen (1994a). One money or many? Analyzing the prospects for Monetary Unification in various parts of the world, *Princeton Studies in International Finance*, no.76.

Bayoumi, T. and B. Eichengreen (1994b). Macroeconomic adjustment under Bretton Woods and the post-Bretton Woods float: an impulse-response analysis, *Economic Journal*, vol.104, no.425, pp.813-827.

Bayoumi, T. and B. Eichengreen (1997). Ever closer to heaven? An optimum-currency-area index for European countries, *European Economic Review*, vol.41, no.3-5, pp.761-770.

Bayoumi, T.; B. Eichengreen and J. von Hagen (1997). European monetary unification: implications of research for policy, implications of policy for research, *Open Economies Review*, 8, pp.71-91.

Beine, M., B. Candelon and A. Hecq (2000). Assessing a perfect European optimum currency area: a common cycles approach, *Empirica*, vol.27, pp.115-132.

Blanchard, O. J. and L. F. Katz (1992). Regional evolutions, *Brookings Papers on Economic Activity*, 1/92, pp.1-75.

Blaug, M. (1992). *The methodology of economics: or how do economists explain*, Cambridge, Cambridge University Press, 2nd ed.

Bofinger, P. (1995), The political economy of the Eastern enlargement of the EU, *CEPR Discussion Paper* no.1234.

Brada, J.C. and J.A. Méndez (1993). Political and economic factors in regional economic integration, *KYKLOS*, vol.46, no.2, pp.183-201.

Brakman, S. and H. Garrettsen (1993). The relevance of initial conditions for the German unification, *KYKLOS*, vol.46, fasc.2, pp.163-181.

Branson, W. H. and J. Brada de Macedo (1995). Macroeconomic policy in Central Europe, *CEPR Discussion Paper*, no.1195.

Britton, A. and D. Mayes (1990). Obstacles to the use of ECU: macroeconomic aspects, *Economic Journal*, vol.100, pp.947-958.

Buigues, P. and F. Ilzkovitz (1992). *Central and Eastern European Countries Basic Facts and Main Issues: Trade*, Commission of the European Communities, DOC.II/125/92-EN.

Button, K. J. and E. J. Pentecost (1995). testing for convergence of the EU regional economies, *Economic Inquiry*, vol.33, no.4, pp.664-671.

Casella, A. (1992). Participation in a currency union, *American Economic Review*, vol.82, no.4, pp.847-863.

CEPR (1993). Annual Report: Making sense of subsidiarity: how much centralisation for Europe?, *Monitoring European Integration*, no.4.

Cohen, B. J (1993). Beyond EMU: the problems of sustainability, *Economics and Politics*, vol.5, no.2, pp.187-203.

Commission of the European Communities (1985). Guidelines for a Community policy on migration, *Bulletin of the European Communities*, no.9.

Commission of the European Communities (1990). One market, one money, *European Economy*, no.44.

Corden, W. M. (1994). *Economic policy, exchange rates and the international system*, Oxford University Press.

Cukierman, A., S. B. Webb and B. Neyapti (1992). Measuring the independence of central banks and its effects on policy outcomes, *World Bank Economic Review*, vol.6, no.3, pp.353-398.

Daviddi, R. and F. Ilzkovitz (1997). The Eastern enlargement of the European Union: major challenges for macro-economic policies and institutions of Central and East European countries, *European Economic Review*, vol.41, no.3-5, pp.671-680.

De Grauwe, P. (1993). The political economy of Monetary Union in Europe, *CEPR Discussion Paper* no.824.

De Grauwe, P. (1994a), Towards EMU without EMS, *Economic Policy*, no.18, pp.149-185.

De Grauwe, P. (1994b). *The economics of monetary integration*, Oxford University Press.

De Grauwe, P. (1995a). Alternative strategies towards Monetary Union, *European Economic Review*, no.39, pp.483-491.

De Grauwe, Paul (1995b), The economics of convergence towards monetary union in Europe, *CEPR Discussion Paper*, no.1213.

De Grauwe, P. (1996). Monetary Union and convergence economics, *European Economic Review*, vol.40, pp.1091-1101.

De Grauwe, P. (1997). *The economics of monetary integration*, 3rd ed., Oxford University Press.

De Nardis, S., A. Goglio and M. Malgarini (1996). Regional specialization and shocks in Europe: some evidence from regional data, *Weltwirtschaftliches Archiv*, vol.132, no.2, pp.197-214.

Dluhosch, B. (2000). *Industrial location and economic integration: centrifugal and centripetal forces in the new Europe*, Edward Elgar.

Douven, R.C. and J.C. Engwerd (1993). Is there room for convergence in the EC?, *CentER for Economic Research Discussion Paper*, no.9350.

Dunn, L. F.; G.S. Maddala (1996). Extracting economic information from data: methodology in an empirical discipline, in: S. G. Medema and W. J. Samuels (eds.), *Foundations of research in economics: how do economists do economics*, London, Edward Elgar.

Dyson, K. (1994). *Elusive Union: the process of economic and monetary union in Europe*, Longman.

Economist (1999). *Europe after communism: Ten years since the wall fell*, November.

Economist (2001). *Work in progress: a survey of European business and the euro*, December.

Eichengreen, B. (1990a). One money for Europe? Lessons from the US currency union, *Economic Policy*, no.10, April.

Eichengreen, B. (1990b). Is Europe an optimum currency area?, *CEPR Discussion Paper*, no.478, November.

Eichengreen B. (1993). Labour markets and European Monetary Unification, in P. R. Masson and M. P. Taylor (eds.), *Policy issues in the operation of currency unions*, Cambridge.

Eichengreen, B. and J. Frieden (1993). The political economy of European monetary unification: an analytical introduction, *Economics and Politics*, vol.5, no.2, pp.85-103.

Eichengreen, B. and F. Ghironi (1995). European Monetary unification: the challenges ahead, *CEPR Discussion Paper*, no.1217.

Euromonitor (1995). *European and Marketing Data Statistics*.

European Commission (1995). *Bulletin of the European Union*, 12.

European Commission (1997). Agenda 2000: For a stronger and wider Union, *Bulletin of the European Union*, Supplement, 5/97.

*** *Europinion* (1996). No.8, March.

Eurostat (1993). International migration in the EU member states in1992: population and social conditions, *Statistics in Focus*, no.3.

Eurostat (1995). *Basic Statistics of the European Union*, 32nd ed.

Evans, P. and G. Karras (1996). Convergence revisited, *Journal of Monetary Economics*, vol.37, pp.249-265.

Fischer, S. (1981). *Towards an understanding of the costs of inflation: II*, Carnagerie-Rochester Conference Series on Public Policy, no.15.

*** *Flash Eurobarometer* (1995). 16-20 December.

Fleming, J. M. (1971). On exchange rate unification, *Economic Journal*, vol.81, no.323, pp.467-488.

Fox, G. (1997). *Reason and reality in the methodologies of economics: an introduction*, Edward Elgar

Frankel, J. and A. Rose (1998). The endogeneity of the optimum currency area criteria, *Economic Journal*, vol.108, no.449, pp.1009-1020.

Friedman, M. (1968) The role of monetary policy, *American Economic Review*, vol.58, no.1, pp.1-17.

Friedman, M (1994). The methodology of positive economics in D. M. Hausman (ed.), *The philosophy of economics: an anthology*, 2nd ed., Cambridge University Press.

Garret, G. (1993). The politics of Maastricht, *Economics and Politics*, vol.5, no.2, pp.105-123.

Genberg, H. and F. Nadal De Simone (1993). Regional integration agreements and macroeconomic discipline, in: K. Anderson and R. Blackhurst (eds.), *Regional integration and the global trading system*, Harvester Wheatsheaf.

Gerlach, S. (1995). Adjustable pegs vs. single currencies: how valuable is the option to realign?, *European Economic Review*, no.39, pp.1155-1170.

Goodhart, C. (1991). An assessment of EMU, *Royal Bank of Scotland Review*, no.170, pp.3-25.

Goodhart, C. (1996). European Monetary Integration, *European Economic Review*, vol.40, pp.1083-1090.

Gouriéroux, C., A. Monfort and E. Renault (1995). Inference in factor models, in G.S. Maddala, Peter C.B. Phillips, T.N. Srinivasan (eds.), *Advances in Econometrics*, Blackwell.

Greenaway, D. and D. Sapsford (1994). What does export liberlization do for exports and growth?, *Weltwirtschaftliches Archiv*, vol.130, no.1, pp.152-173.

Grilli, V., D. Masciandaro and G. Tabellini (1991)., Political and monetary institutions and public financial policies in the industrial countries, *Economic Policy*, no.13, pp.341-392.

Gros, D. (1996). A reconsideration of the optimum currency area approach: the role of external shocks and labour mobility, *National Institute Economic Review*, no.158, pp.108-117.

Gros, D. and N. Thygesen (1990). The institutional approach to monetary union in Europe, *Economic Journal*, vol.100, no.402, pp.925-935.

Gros, D. and N. Thygesen (1992). *European Monetary Integration*, Longman.

Hansen, J. D., H. Heinrich and J. U. M. Nielsen (1992). *An economic analysis of the EC*, McGraw Hill.

Harrop, J. (1992). *The political economy of integration in the European Community*, 2nd ed., Edward Elgar.

Hoekman, B. and S. Djankov (1996). Intra-industry trade, foreign direct investment and the reorientation of East European exports, *CEPR Discussion Paper*, no.1377.

Hofstede, G. (1990). Motivation, leadership and organisation: do American theories apply abroad?, in: Pugh D.S. (ed), *Organisational theory: selected readings*, Penguin Books.

Hopkinson, N. (1994). The Eastern enlargement of the European Union, *Wilton Park Paper*, no.91.

Hugues Hallet, A.J. and D. Vines (1993). On the possible costs of EMU, *Manchester School of Economic and Social Studies*, vol.61, no.1, pp.35-64.

Inotai, A. (2000). Political, economic and social arguments in favour of and against enlargement of the European Union: a review of influential pressure groups, *European Urban and Regional Studies*, vol.7, pp.269-280.

Ishiyama, Y. (1975). The theory of optimum currency areas: a survey, *IMF Staff Papers*, July.

Johnson, H.G. (1965). An economic theory of protectionism, tariff bargaining and the formation of Customs Unions, *Journal of Political Economy*, vol.73, pp.256-283.

Johnson, R. A. and D. W. Wichern (1992). *Applied multivariate statistical analysis*, 3rd ed., Prentice Hall.

Jolliffe, I.T., B. Jones and B.J.T. Morgan (1995). Identifying influential observations in hierarchical cluster analysis, *Journal of Applied Statistics*, vol.22, no.1, pp.61-80.

Kaplan, A. (1964). *The conduct of inquiry: methodology for behavioural science*, San Francisco, Chandler Publishing Company.

Kenen, P. (1969). The theory of optimum currency areas: an eclectic view, in R. A. Mundell and A. K. Swoboda (eds.), *Monetary problems of the international economy*, The University of Chicago Press.

Knell, M. (1995). Towards European integration: is Eastern Europe catching up or falling behind?, *De Montfort University (Leicester) Discussion Papers in Economics*, no.95-18.

Kokko, A. (1994). Sweden: effects of EU membership on investment and growth, *World Economy*, vol.17, no.5, pp.667-677.

Krugman, P. (1981). Intra-industry specialisation and the gains from trade, *Journal of Political Economy*, vol.89, pp.959-973.

Krugman, P. (1990). Policy problems of a monetary union, in: De Grauwe, P. and L. Papademos (eds.), *The European Monetary System in the 1990s*, London, Longman.

Krugman, P. (1991). *Geography and trade*, Leuven University Press and MIT Press.

Krzanowski, W.J. (1996). *Principles of multivariate analysis: a user's perspective*, Oxford, Clarendon Press.

Little, R. J. A. and D. B. Rubin (1987). *Statistical analysis with missing data*, New York, Wiley&Sons.

Lundberg, L. (1994). Finland: economics and politics of EU accession: a comment, *World Economy*, vol.17, no.5, pp.715-718.

Machlup, F. (1978). *Methodology of economics and other social sciences*, New York, Academic Press.

Maes, I. (1996). The development of economic thought at the European Community Institutions, *typescript*.

Mansfield, E. D. (1993). Effects of international politics on regionalism in international trade, in: K. Anderson and R. Blackhurst (eds.), *Regional integration and the global trading system*, Harvester Wheatsheaf.

Martín, C. (1995). The impact of EU Trade Agreements with Central and East European countries: the case of Spain, *CEPR Discussion Paper*, no.1238.

Martin, L. L. (1993). International and domestic institutions in the EMU process, *Economics and Politics*, vol.5, no.2, pp.125-143.

Masson, P. R. and M. P. Taylor (1993). Currency unions: a survey of the issues, in P. R. Masson and M. P. Taylor (eds.), *Policy Issues in the operation of currency areas*, Cambridge University Press.

McKibbin, W. J. and T. Bok (1994). Which monetary regime for Europe? A quantitative evaluation, *typescript*.

McKinnon, R. J (1963). Optimum currency areas, *American Economic Review*, September, vol.53, no.4, pp.717-725.

McKinnon, R. J (1973). The dual currency system revisited, in H. G. Johnson and A. K. Swoboda (eds.), *The economics of common currencies: proceedings of the Madrid Conference on Optimum Currency Areas*, London, George Allen & UNWIN Ltd.

McKinnon, R. J (1994). A common monetary standard or a common currency for Europe? Fiscal lessons from the United States, *Scottish Journal of Political Economy*, vol.41, no.4, pp.337-357.

Mélitz, J (1995a). The current impasse in research on OCAs, *European Economic Review*, vol.39, no.3-4, pp.492-500.

Mélitz, J (1995b). A suggested reformulation of the theory of OCAs - review essay, *Open Economies Review*, vol.6, no.3, pp.281-298.

Mélitz, J (1995c). The future of European monetary integration, *University of St. Andrews (Scotland) Department of Economics Occasional Paper*, no.9506.

Milligan, G. W. (1981). A review of Monte Carlo tests of cluster analysis, *Multivariate Behavioural Research*, vol.16, pp.379-407.

Mundell, R. A. (1961). A theory of optimum currency areas, *American Economic Review*, September, vol.51, no.4, pp.657-665.

Nesselroade, J. R. (1994). Exploratory factor analysis with latent variables and the study of processes of development and change in Von Eye, A. and C.C. Clogg (eds.), *Latent variables analysis: applications for developmental research*, Sage Publications.

Norušis, Marija J. (1985). *SPSS X: advanced statistics guide*, New York, McGraw-Hill.

Norušis, Marija J. (1994). *SPSS Professional Statistics 6.1*,Chicago, SPSS Inc.

Papagni, E. (1992). High-technology exports of EEC countries: persistence and diversity of specialisation patterns, *Applied Economics*, vol.24, pp.925-933.

Pelkmans, J. (1998). *European integration: methods of economic analysis*, Longman.

Persson, T. (1988). Credibility of macroeconomic policy: an introduction and broad survey, *European Economic Review*, vol.32, no.2/3, pp.519-532.

Porojan, A. (2001). Who Gains From Monetary Union? An Estimate of Relative Net Benefits for EU15 Member States, *Journal of European Integration,* 2001, vol. 23, issue 3, pp.281-302.

Prud'homme, R. (1993). The potential role of the EC budget on the reduction of spatial disparities in a European Economic and Monetary Union, *European Economy*, no.5, pp.317-351.

Quah, D. T. (1996). Regional convergence clusters across Europe, *European Economic Review*, vol.40, pp.951-958.

Razin, A. and C. W. Yuen (1996). Labour mobility and fiscal coordination: setting growth agenda for an economic union, *CEPR Discussion Paper*, no.1342.

Reuten, G. (1998). Dialectical method, in J. B. David, D. W. Hands and U. Mäki (eds.), *The handbook of economic methodology*, Edward Elgar.

Robson, Peter (1998), *The economics of international integration*, 4th ed., Routledge: London.

Rubin, D. B. and H. S. Stern (1994). Testing in latent class models using a posterior predictive check distribution, in Von Eye, A. and C.C. Clogg (eds.), *Latent variables analysis: applications for developmental research*, Sage Publications.

Rudden, B. and D. Wyatt (eds.) (1994). *Basic Community Laws*, 5th ed., Oxford, Clarendon Press.

Rummel, R. J. (1970). *Applied factor analysis*, Northern University Press.

Sala-i-Martin, X. and J. Sachs, (1992). Fiscal federalism and optimum currency areas: evidence for Europe from the United States, in M. B. Canzoneri, V. Grilli and P. R. Masson (eds.), *Establishing a central bank: issues in Europe for lessons from the US*, Cambridge University Press.

Samuels, W. J. and A. A. Schmid (1997). The concept of cost in economics, in W. J. Samuels, S. G. Medema and A. A. Schmid (eds.), *The economy as a process of Valuation*, Cheltenham, Edward Elgar.

Sibert, A. (1994). The allocation of seigniorage in a common currency area, *Journal of International Economics*, vol.37, no.1/2, pp.111-122.

Smith, J. (2002). Enlarging the European Union, *Journal of Common Market Studies*, vol.40, pp.117-120.

Sobel, M. E. (1994). Causal influence in latent variable models, in Von Eye, A. and C.C. Clogg (eds.), *Latent variables analysis: applications for developmental research*, Sage Publications.

Spaventa, L. (1996). Out in the cold? Outsiders and insiders in 1999: feasible and unfeasible options, *CEPR Discussion Paper* no.1379.

Spilimbergo, A. and E. Stein (1996). The welfare implications of trading blocs among countries with different endowments, *NBER Working Paper*, no.5472.

Srinivasan, T.N.; J. Whalley and I. Wooton (1993). Measuring the effects of regionalism on trade and welfare, in: K. Anderson and R. Blackhurst (eds.), *Regional integration and the global trading system*, Harvester Wheatsheaf.

Stone, R (1951). *The role of measurement in economics*, Cambridge University Press.

Sverdrup, U. (2002). An institutional perspective on treaty reform: contextualizing the Amsterdam and Nice Treaties, *Journal of European Public Policy*, vol.9, no.1, pp.120-140.

Tabachnick, B. G. and L. S. Fidell (1996). *Using multivariate statistics*, 3rd ed., Harper Collins.

Tavlas, G. (1993). The 'new' theory of optimum currency areas, *World Economy*, vol.16, no.6, pp.663-685.

Tinbergen, J. (1952). *On the theory of economic policy*, Amsterdam, North Holland.

Tower, E. and T. D. Willett (1976). The theory of optimum currency areas and exchange-rate flexibility, *Special Papers In International Economics*, no.11, Princeton.

Tukey, J. W. (1980). We need both exploratory and confirmatory, *American Statistician*, vol.34, no.1, pp.23-25.

Urwin, D. W. (1991). *The Community of Europe: a history of European integration since 1945*, London, Longman.

Usher, J. (1994). *The law of money and financial services in the European Community*, Oxford, Clarendon Press.

Van De Geer, J. P. (1971). *Introduction to multivariate analysis for the social sciences*, WH Freeman.

Vanthoor, W. F.V. (1996). *European Monetary Union since 1848: a political and historical analysis*, Cheltenham, Edward Elgar.

Varian, H. R. (1996). What use is economic theory?, in S. G. Medema and W. J. Samuels (eds.), *Foundations of research in economics*, London, Edward Elgar.

Vaubel, R. (1990). Currency competition and European monetary integration, *Economic Journal*, vol.100, pp.936-946.

Viñals, J. (1996). European monetary integration: a narrow or a wide EMU?, *European Economic Review*, vol.40, pp.1103-1109.

Viner, J (1950). *The customs union issue*, Stevens & Sons.

Von Hagen, J. and M. Fratianni (1993). The transition to European Monetary Union and the European Monetary Institute, *Economics and Politics*, vol.5, no.2, pp.167-185.

Wijkman, P. M. (1992). The European Free Trade Area expanded? The European Community, EFTA and Eastern Europe, *EFTA Occasional Paper*, no.43.

Winkler, B. (1995). Reputation for EMU: an economic defence of the Maastricht criteria, *European University Institute (EUI-Florence) Working Paper* ECO no.95/18.

Winters, L. A. (1993). Expanding EC membership and association accords: recent experience and future prospects, in: K. Anderson and R. Blackhurst (eds.), *Regional integration and the global trading system*, Harvester Wheatsheaf.

INDEX

F

G

H

I

J

K

L

M

N

O

P

R

S

T

U

V

W